THE

SAVAGE

NUMBER

THE
SAVAGE
NUMBER

HOW MUCH
MONEY DO YOU
NEED TO RETIRE?

TERRY SAVAGE

WILEY

John Wiley & Sons, Inc.

Published by John Wiley & Sons, Inc., Hoboken, New Jersey.
Published simultaneously in Canada.

For general information about our other products and services, please contact our Customer Care Department within the United States at 800-762-2974, outside the United States at 317-572-3993 or fax 317-572-4002.

Wiley also publishes its books in a variety of electronic formats. Some content that appears in print may not be available in electronic books. For more information about Wiley products, visit our web site at www.wiley.com.

Library of Congress Cataloging-in-Publication Data:

Savage, Terry.
  The Savage number : how much money do you need to retire? / Terry Savage.
    p. cm.
  ISBN-13 978-0-471-72799-6 (cloth)
  ISBN-10 0-471-72799-7 (cloth)
  ISBN-13 978-0-470-06774-1 (pbk.)
  ISBN-10 0-470-06774-8 (pbk.)
  1. Retirement income—Planning 2. Finance, Personal. I. Title.
    HG179.S2396   2005
    332.024'014—dc22

                                                                    2005003021

10 9 8 7 6 5 4 3 2

Grow old along with me!
The best is yet to be,
The last of life, for which the first was made . . .
—Robert Browning

For hah!

CONTENTS

Part 2   Monte Carlo Your Money

Part 5   Long-Term Care: The Greatest Risk of All

THE
SAVAGE
NUMBER

INTRODUCTION

Can You Retire?

You want a simple answer to your most important financial question: *How much money do I need to retire?* And then you have one more question: *How much money can I spend every month and not run out of money before I run out of time?*

Well, let me ask *you* a few questions:

- At what age do you want to retire?
- How much money have you saved already?
- How much money do you think you'll need every month for living expenses?
- What's your estimate for the inflation rate during your retirement years?
- What's your risk tolerance for investments?
- And by the way, how long do you think you'll live?

If you knew those answers for sure, retirement planning would be easy. But life is filled with uncertainty. That's no excuse for avoiding the issue.

A quick search of the Internet on the subject of retirement calculators offers nearly one hundred web sites, mostly from financial services companies and financial planning firms. They will instantly calculate how much money you need to retire based on your answers to those basic questions. The amounts may be intimidating.

One of the best online calculators is the "Ballpark Estimate Worksheet" at **www.choosetosave.org**. It will show you how much you *should* be saving every month. You can use the Society of Actuaries' Retirement Probability analyzer, available at **www.soa.org** to get a more sophisticated analysis of how long your nest egg is likely to last.

But you'll need more than these calculators to plan for a successful retirement. You need personalized advice about how to invest your money along the way. And you'll need a withdrawal plan that ensures you won't run out of money before you run out of time.

Now that kind of personalized advice is within reach of the average American, in a format that is not only understandable and practical, but individual. It's called Monte Carlo modeling, but it has nothing to do with gambling. Quite the contrary. It's a very exacting analysis of probabilities. And it's the basis for making informed decisions about our retirement finances.

The *Savage Number*—how much money you need to retire—is a personal and unique number, but it is knowable. It comes with advice on getting *to* the number, as well as getting *through* your retirement years with enough money to cover foreseeable expenses. In fact, the Savage Number is readily available to you, at no cost but your willingness to think about it and accept help. It will take more than a few minutes and a few mouse clicks, but it will be well worth your time.

You've seen the familiar headlines: Baby boomers can't afford to retire! You can respond in one of two ways: (1) You can refuse to think about it, or (2) you can take time to figure out your options and get help. Believe me, getting good help with retirement planning is easier and less expensive than you think. The whole point of this book is to show you the way.

The entire financial services industry is gearing up to serve *you,* the baby boomer approaching retirement. For the past decade, mutual funds, banks, and brokers have been trying to get you to invest. Now they're trying to help you retire.

You may not have a lot of money saved. In fact, you may not have saved anything. You may be living with credit card debt. Time marches on, even if your investments don't. And at some point in the future, you're going to want to retire, or your job will retire from you.

What does the word *retire* mean? Each of us will have our own definition. For some, it's a full-time vacation in a sunny spot near a golf course. For many more, it will be a part-time job to maintain a reasonable standard of living. And for some, it will be dependence on programs like Social Security and Medicare.

Odds are we'll live longer than our parents will. And odds are they'll use up all their money living longer than they planned. So we won't have an inheritance to rescue us. And odds are our children—for those who have them—won't want to spend their scarce dollars taking care of us.

Should we be scared? Absolutely not. We're the generation that grew up in the shadow of the Cold War and the Soviet Union; nuclear fears and the Doomsday Clock; unprecedented inflation that spawned a 21 percent prime interest rate and 15 percent mortgage rates; the worst recession (in 1980–1982) since the Great Depression; the biggest bear market since the crash of 1929; and the worst terrorist attack on our country since Pearl Harbor.

We've survived all that. Certainly we can survive retirement! And we can do it in style, if we start thinking about it now—thinking about the balance between living our lives to the fullest today and giving ourselves a chance at the lifestyle we want in the future. Small steps taken now, while we are earning our best income and in good health, can make all the difference. Those steps may cost more in attention than they do in dollars—hence the term "paying attention."

Baby boomers have always changed America, and we're about to do it again. It doesn't take magic. We have computer technology on our side. It will provide the Savage Number, which, along with self-discipline, will bring us to our own secure retirement.

PART 1

RETRO-RETIREMENT

CHAPTER 1

THE SAVAGE NUMBER

The subject of retirement both beckons and repels. We may avoid thinking about it because we assume we can't make our dreams come true or because we're too busy surviving the present to worry about the future. Or maybe we fool ourselves into thinking that something will come along to save us. After all, it always has. But at the back of our mind is that lingering worry: How can I possibly retire?

Thinking about the Savage Number can be overwhelming. It includes not just the money you need in order to retire, but also the money you must continue earning—either on your investments or by other income—while you are *in* retirement. It involves deciding how much you can withdraw to spend and still make your money last as long as you do. And it carries the responsibility of investing to meet your goals amidst uncertainty about everything from inflation to health-care needs.

Retirement will take on an entirely different meaning for the baby boomer generation. We'll live longer, need more money, have less security from Social Security, pay more for medical expenses, and generally face more financial challenges than any other generation. Retirement no longer means whiling away a few years in a golfing community or enjoying the sun on a park bench, as it may have for our parents or grandparents. Longevity adds to uncertainty.

But don't fear. Just as the baby boomers redefined society from kindergarten to college to the job market, the power of this huge generation will redesign retirement. We will work longer, though probably at different jobs than our life careers. We will be flexible about our lifestyles and more concerned about our health than about our material possessions.

Boomers chose the Beatles and the Rolling Stones. Boomers were fueled by McDonald's and Coke. And, in turn, companies that catered to boomers became profitable investments. That will happen again, as retiring boomers demand new products and services. Because of its size, the boomer generation will always impact the economy. And the economy will find a way to accommodate us.

Boomers are reaching age 50 at a rate of more than 12,000 a day—one person every eight seconds. That statistic comes from AARP—the organization that sends you a birthday greeting and a membership application on the day you turn 50. They should know!

Over the next decade, the 76 million members of the baby boomer generation will start reaching the traditional retirement age of 65. Today, there are 35 million Americans over the age of 65. By 2025, that number will nearly double, as you can see in Figure 1.1. Seniors will comprise a voting pool with more clout than ever.

That power of the baby boomer generation will last a long time because people are living longer. Today, when a man reaches age 65, his life expectancy is another 16.3 years. A 65-year-old woman today can expect to live another 19.2 years. But those are just averages. That means half of us will live longer, and half won't make it that far. And we'll never know in advance which half we fall into. We worry when we hear of friends dying from cancer or suffering with infirmities. Suddenly we feel our mortality. But statistics show that the fastest growing population cohort is people over age 100. You might be one of them!

We can assume, on average, that we'll live longer than our parents because of advances in medical science that prolong life. And given our influence, we'll be heard in the halls of Congress when we demand more attention to our needs—from nursing homes to drug benefits.

Percent
Change

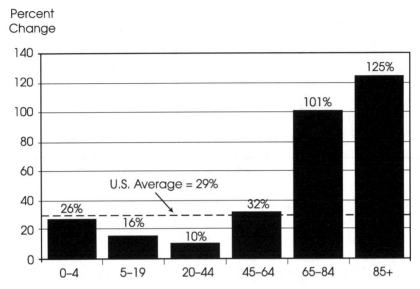

Figure 1.1   The U.S. Is Aging: Projected Change in Population by Age Group, 2000-2030
Source: Milken Institute. Reprinted with permission.

Avoiding Generation Warfare

But government can't take care of us if the younger generations refuse to be taxed to pay for it. Unless we plan for our own secure future, we risk creating generation warfare in the United States. If your own children aren't willing to take care of you, how can you expect other people's children to do the job through their tax dollars?

It's not just a question of morality. Even in a growing economy, there simply won't be enough of the next generation to support us *and* educate their own children. During the baby boomers' peak working years, 1980 to 2000, there were almost four people of working age for every one person over age 65. But as we boomers retire, that ratio will shift. By 2035, there will be fewer than three people working for each person over 65. And remember that those workers—our children—will be trying to care for their own families on what remains of their paychecks after taxes.

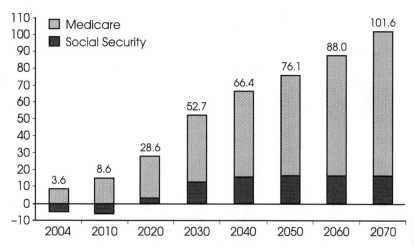

Figure 1.2   Percentage of Income Tax Revenues Needed to Meet the Payroll Tax Shortfall on Social Security and Medicare
Source: National Center for Policy Analysis (NCPA). Calculations based on data from the 2004 Medicare and Social Security Trustees Reports. Reprinted with permission.

As you can see in Figure 1.2, unless cuts are made in government programs, retiree benefits will soon consume the majority of our tax revenues, leaving little for defense, education, or other national needs. According to the trustees of the Medicare program, by 2019, 24 percent of all income tax revenues will be needed for the Medicare program. The curve grows exponentially. By 2040, 51 percent of all income tax revenues will have to go to Medicare. Social Security trust funds are expected to have a negative outflow of cash by 2017—and to become insolvent by 2041.

Actually, Social Security has for many years been a system of transfer payments. Even as you get a statement from Social Security listing your contributions and promised benefits, you should realize that those benefits are being funded each year out of general tax revenues. There is no trust fund, no shoebox in Baltimore with your money inside it. The deduction from your paycheck this week will pay for a retiree's check next month.

Together, Social Security and Medicare taxes are expected to fall $550 billion a year short of covering the programs' expenses in

2018—and the gap will grow larger every year after that. By the time the youngest boomers retire, the shortfall could be $3.7 trillion.

Social Security is likely to undergo major changes before or during your retirement. The benefits you expect to receive will be postponed to a later retirement age—and could even be means-tested—to keep those payments from sinking the entire federal budget. Social Security is *not* your safety net. And no matter how much you've saved for your retirement, the biggest hole in your personal safety net is the rising cost of health care.

Medicare cannot continue to fund the current level of health benefits—including the newest treatments and prescription drug benefits—for this growing population of seniors. Don't look to your previous employer for help. Companies are cutting back on retiree health benefits at a time when costs for medical services are rising twice as fast as traditional measures of consumer price inflation.

Neither Medicare nor Social Security covers the cost of long-term custodial care, either in your own home or in a nursing home, except for a very limited number of days after a hospitalization. Government tries to provide custodial care for impoverished seniors through state-run Medicaid programs, but the facilities that offer that care will be sorely strained by the huge boomer generation. Planning to become impoverished by gifting assets to your children so that Medicaid will cover your care is a recipe for disaster. You'll give up the freedom of choice you get when you purchase long-term care insurance to cover those costs.

Some people are hoping that the government will simply print enough money to fund the promised government retirement benefits. But creating more money through inflation destroys the value of everything you've saved. We learned that lesson in the 1970s, when the government tried to create enough new money to have both guns and butter. We certainly don't want our government to try to give us both bridges and benefits in 2030, just when both are wearing thin!

Government is not the solution. It will contribute, but not enough. Even some corporate pension promises are being called into question. It's up to us to rearrange current lifestyles and expectations for the future. And we have to do it now, while we have flexibility.

HOPING FOR A MIRACLE?

There will be no miracle solutions to make your retirement dreams come true—not the government, the stock market, the family home, or a windfall inheritance.

For a while, it seemed like the stock market would bail out boomers' retirement dreams. Employees were admonished for decades to save and invest money in company retirement plans or individual retirement accounts, but many failed to do so. Those who did had unrealistic expectations. The stock market crash early in this century destroyed their hopes that outsized investment returns would offset a lack of diligence in savings. If history is a guide, stock market investments should outperform other alternatives over the long run—at least 20 years. Even if there are reasons to believe that stock market returns might lag their historical trend lines in the next decade or so, as you'll see in Chapter 8, that's not an argument to stay away from stocks. In fact, it's the reverse: You'll need even more exposure to equities in your retirement investment assets.

More recent hopes for a financial miracle have rested on residential real estate, but real estate is a market just like stocks—and far less liquid. By now, you should have learned that when any market's gains exceed historic trends, the bubble will burst. Even if you sell the family home at a substantial profit, there are taxes to be paid and reinvestment decisions to be made. Then you'll still need a place to live. Reverse mortgages may be one answer, as explained in Chapter 14.

And forget about inheriting money from your parents. According to AARP, by the start of 2002, baby boomers who had received an inheritance received a median of just under $48,000. Those who received much more than that were wealthier to begin with. Almost two-thirds of inheritances went to families with a net worth of about $150,000. As parents live longer and spend more, inheritances will dwindle. In fact, many boomers will need to provide financial assistance to their aging parents.

There are additional factors beyond our control. The Employee Benefit Research Institute's latest retirement confidence survey gives one more unsettling statistic. In 2004, about 37 percent of retirees left the workforce earlier than they had planned. The causes were divided among health problems, disability, and changes at their company, such as downsizing and closure.

You're Not Alone

An annual survey of preretirees done by Metropolitan Life Insurance Company finds that there is a national crisis in retirement planning because so many preretirees have misconceptions about issues affecting their retirement. People tend to underestimate savings requirements, life expectancy, and the rising cost of health care, while overestimating how much they can draw on their savings. Even small miscalculations of those numbers can result in huge errors.

The Employee Benefit Research Institute survey shows that 45 percent of all workers report total household assets, excluding the value of their home, of less than $25,000. In spite of all the publicity given to the need for retirement savings, the survey shows that only about 60 percent of workers say they are currently saving for retirement.

Worrying about retirement is fodder for cartoons. There are just so many uncertainties: how long you'll live, how much your money can earn, the rate at which inflation will eat away at your savings, and the rising costs of health care. The challenge of planning for retirement may seem overwhelming, but you have to face reality. Will you ever be able to save enough to fund a secure retirement? If saving more isn't possible, and if extraordinary investment returns are unrealistic, then working longer—either longer *hours* now or longer *years* later—may be the only alternative. That will allow the money you currently have in savings and investments to grow for a few extra years while you set aside a few more years of retirement plan contributions. Even a few years of additional contributions and delayed withdrawals can make a big difference.

But that may not be enough. It's time to reexamine the entire concept of retirement.

Pepper . . . and Salt

THE WALL STREET JOURNAL

"The financial strategy for my retirement should count on me still being alive."

Source: From the *Wall Street Journal*—permission, cartoon features syndicate.

THE LIKELY SOLUTION: RETRO-RETIREMENT

Have you noticed that what's old is new again? It's happening in fashion, where 20-year-olds are adopting the styles you wore in the 1960s. What a shame you can't still fit into those bell-bottom jeans, pointed-toe shoes, or wide-lapel jackets! Today, those clothes are called "vintage." Young career women are paying good money for the stuff we gave away. Even furniture and car designs have become retro-chic. It seems to take a couple of generations before everything old becomes new. So what's wrong with a retro-retirement? It's time to take a new look at a vintage idea and give it our own modern twist.

Think about it. Your grandparents, and their parents, worked until they died. They didn't complain. That's just the way it was. Even the stock exchange was open on Saturday, until 1952. Their recreation took place on Sunday. It wasn't until the late twentieth century that your parents' generation came up with the idea of retirement built around the concept of working less, or not at all, while living on a pension—an unending stream of income that would subsidize their lifestyle. Suddenly, workers could buy recreational vehicles, mobile homes, and cottages at the lake. Our higher standards of living were extended into retirement years.

But in the new reality, we're living longer and it's costing more. Maybe it's sour grapes, but boomers who have worked all their lives might find it a bit boring to play golf or tennis, to sit on the beach, or to drive across the country. We're creating our own concept of retirement that will be every bit as defining of our generation as the Beatles and the Rolling Stones. We'll work and we'll play on our own schedule. It will be retro-chic to do both—and to do them in style.

It's not impossible for boomers to retire, but we must redefine the term. Almost certainly, it will involve working longer. But then we'll be living longer. Health care may cost more, but we'll probably be healthier than our parents. We may have less money, but we'll have a better chance to enjoy what we have. It all starts with facing up to the choices.

THE STARTING POINT

These three questions require no specific knowledge to answer, but a lot of self-discipline and honesty. There are no right or wrong answers.

1. How old do I expect to be when I die? _____
2. How do I rank the following three retirement solutions?
   Working longer before retiring _____
   Lowering standard of living in retirement_____
   Saving more now _____
3. If I knew I could get trustworthy advice about how to save, invest, budget, and withdraw, I'd be willing to confront the financial issues of retirement. _____ (yes or no)

With so much uncertainty, how can anyone know the Savage Number? Well, here's a helpful thought: You don't have to hit the number right on the head. Getting close counts more in retirement than in horseshoes!

CHAPTER 2

TIME IS MONEY

et's overcome the first objection to retirement planning: *I don't have enough time.* Get over it. There will never be enough time to do all the things you want to do, to make all the money you want to make, to enjoy all the things life has to offer. The secret is to make use of the time you have, starting right this minute.

Time is money. If you're like most people, you feel you don't have enough of either. And you're probably right. But if you were asked to choose between the two, your answer would be revealing. If you choose time, it means you've reached the point in life where realities change. You understand this simple truth: *Time can buy you money, but no amount of money can buy you time.*

And that understanding colors the way you look at your future. Time has become a finite commodity. The issue now is to make the most of time and to make sure you have the money to do that, even though you will never know how much time you have left. The challenge is not to count the minutes, but to make the minutes count.

CONSUMING TIME AND MONEY

It's not your imagination that time is flying faster than ever. The days of your childhood, when summer stretched on endlessly, are long behind you. Now the days, months, and years fly by quickly. You ask: Where did all the time go and where did all the money go? Some of the money that slipped through your fingers is all around you. Your home, car, furniture, and clothing are all a reflection of how you spent your working time. Every acquisition has a price, and the price was the time you spent making the money to buy it.

Some of those acquisitions are long gone—clothing that went out of style and was given away, cars that depreciated in value and were sold. Other acquisitions have grown in value. Your education was costly, but it was valuable in creating the ability to earn more money. Your savings and investments, though battered by bear markets, continue to use the leverage of time to grow in value.

Overall, we live in a society that is based on consumption. Neither terrorist acts nor economic recessions have kept the U.S. consumer from shopping and adding to consumer debt. In a recent MetLife trends study, more than half of the respondents reported that they manage their finances by living paycheck to paycheck. (See Figure 2.1.) If that's how you're getting by, you're not alone. It's not surprising that younger employees, ages 21 to 30, have little savings or investments. But it is shocking to find that more than half of older employees, ages 61 to 69, are also waiting for the next paycheck to pay their bills.

If you think this lack of planning is a result of low incomes, think again. Fully one-third (34 percent) of higher-income workers earning $75,000 or more are also dependent on the next paycheck for survival. Thirty percent of those earning $100,000 or more say they're living month to month. All of the people in this survey worked for corporations and were receiving some level of benefits. Half of them said they were worried about outliving their retirement savings.

RUNNING OUT OF TIME

But worrying and doing something about it seem to be mutually exclusive. It's as if Americans are addicted to debt, even though they understand that interest payments limit their ability to plan for a

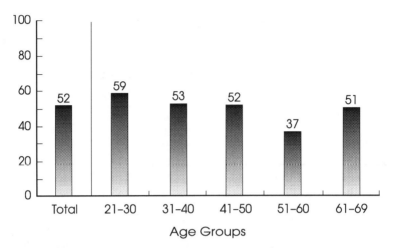

Figure 2.1   Percentage of Respondents Saying They Live Paycheck to Paycheck by Age
Source: Metropolitan Life Insurance Company. Reprinted with permission.

secure future. Bankruptcy has become an epidemic, but even liquidation of debt does not always result in new attitudes toward saving.

It's unthinkable that as the baby boomer generation ages, many of its members will live at a subsistence level. A growing economy will solve many of the problems of supporting an aging population. But an economy can't grow if the government sucks up its resources through higher taxes.

There are many issues filled with uncertainties: How much money is enough? How much time will you have? Is it too late to start? Actually, the answers are easier than you think. Although you can't buy time, you can make better use of your time to add to your retirement savings. It's never too late to start the process.

What's Your Time Worth?

It's critically important to evaluate your personal relationship to time and money—a valuation that will be different for every individual. It's difficult to put a dollar value on a minute, a day, or a year of your time. You can divide your annual after-tax salary by the number of hours you worked. That will give you the dollar value of one hour of your time. But most of us would say we're worth far more than that mathematical calculation—because, of course, we're underpaid!

Still, give it a try. Figure out how many hours you work in an average week, and divide your weekly paycheck by that number. Remember to use the *after-tax* figure for your pay. It's a rough calculation; but you may find your work is worth $20 an hour, $50, $100, or more. Knowing how hard you work to earn your money gives you a new perspective when it comes to spending it.

When you make any purchase, it's worth computing how much of your work time the item would cost. If you take home $50 per hour, then a $250 winter coat will cost you almost one workday. But if your take-home pay is only $25 an hour, the coat will cost you nearly two days of work. Perhaps you could find something less expensive. That new flat-screen high-definition TV at $2,500 will cost you 50 hours of work. Is it worth it? This is not a lesson in budgeting; it's an exercise in valuation, and it will lead you to your own personal conclusions. There is no right or wrong.

The answer to the question "Is it worth it?" will depend not only on the per-hour cost of your time, but on how you will use the item you're buying. In fact, one of my favorite pastimes is computing a "wear quotient." Wearing that $250 winter coat for two years gives a wear quotient of $1 per day ($250 divided by about 250 cold-weather days over two years). But a $250 dress worn twice has a wear quotient of $125. Consider your own wardrobe. You may have a mutual fund full of style but no substance in your closet. Also think about sporting goods, car accessories, or electronics that didn't give you enough use to justify their costs in terms of your time.

Consider the potential impact of time on the money you *don't* spend today. What could have been done with the money instead? It's not always easy to compute the future value of current expenditures. You may go into debt to earn an advanced degree in business that will increase your value to prospective employers. These days, many students graduate from college with student loan debt well over $50,000. It will be up to them to prove the long-term value of their investment in education.

THE TIME VALUE OF MONEY

Another way to value time is to measure how it can make your money grow without any extra input from you. Investing $2,000 a year ($38.46 per week) in an individual retirement account (IRA), growing in a stock index mutual fund at the stock market's historic average rate of slightly over 10 percent, could build a huge retirement fund. Starting today, a 20-year-old could make that annual $2,000 investment inside an IRA for 50 years and have an account worth $3.1 million at retirement! Fully funding an IRA at $4,000 a year could generate a $6 million nest egg in 50 years, if the stock market continues its average performance of the past 75 years. If it's too late for you, tell a young person!

Clearly, the power of compound interest—the impact of time on money—is a major force of nature. The problem is that when you're young, you have no idea that time is such a valuable commodity because you have so much of it. When you're young, money (not time) is the immediately scarce resource. You don't have the long-term perspective until you have hindsight.

Unfortunately, we learn the value of time only when we recognize it is a finite commodity. And it is not only finite, but indefinable. No one gives us a sneak peek at when it will run out. If we knew for sure, it would be easier to plan. Even so, it's never too late to vow to make the very best use of the time we have.

The greatest financial mistake we can make is to waste time. Following are some common time wasters and solutions to help you avoid them.

HOW TO AVOID WASTING TIME (AND MONEY)

Time *can* buy you money—if you stop wasting it.

Time Waster: Worry

If you're nearing retirement and you haven't started saving, you might think it's hopeless. But worrying about money doesn't create more money. It just wastes time you could be using to change your financial situation.

Solution: It's never too late to start a regular program of automatic investing. Have money taken out of your paycheck or checking account before you spend it. Remember, it's quite possible you will live beyond age 85. That gives the money you invest today plenty of time to grow in the future. (See the section titled "Starting Small—No Excuses" in Chapter 10 for ways to start investing with as little as $100.)

Time Waster: Drudgery

Many people confuse the drudgery of money management with the idea that they're taking control of their finances. Paying bills is the perfect example. The time you spend writing and mailing checks each month could be better spent evaluating your retirement plan statement.

Solution: Start paying your bills online with just a click of your mouse. It's safe, it's free (or inexpensive), and it saves time. Go to your bank's web site to get started. For more information on using your computer to eliminate time-wasting money drudgery, see Chapter 6.

Time Waster: Complaining

Complaining about how underpaid, overworked, or unappreciated you are is a horrible waste of time.

Solution: Do something different with your time. Start your own small business on the side, or take a night school course to make yourself more valuable. Volunteering to help others can set you on the path to creating a business that builds on your talents. Invest the time you spend complaining into building your own future.

CHAPTER 3

THE 10 KEY QUESTIONS

et's see where we are so far. Retirement is the goal. You're willing to face the challenge of finding the Savage Number. You tested yourself and realized you'll need some help getting there. You've bought into the principle that time is money. And you're worried about being able to retire.

Don't worry. You're not alone. A study from Forrester Research, Inc., an independent technology research company, shows that 51 percent of baby boomers worry they'll never be able to retire. But you will be able to—if you ask the right questions and know where to get good answers.

So let's get specific about the 10 key questions you'll face in retirement planning. Ask yourself:

1. How long will I live?
2. What will inflation do to the value of my savings?
3. How can I save enough?
4. How should I invest the money I've saved for retirement?
5. How much will I spend to live in retirement?
6. How much can I withdraw each month without running out of money?
7. What's the biggest danger to my retirement plans?
8. How can I earn money during retirement?
9. How can I retain control of my financial life?
10. What if I have money leftover when I die?

Let's take the questions one by one. But keep in mind that while it's easier to explain things in terms of averages, very few things in real life are actually average. It's not averages you need to deal with in retirement planning, but probabilities. They're much more likely to get you to your retirement goal. So the average numbers in this chapter are just designed to give perspective. Dealing with specific probabilities for your retirement plan comes in the next section.

HOW LONG WILL I LIVE?

This is truly the one unanswerable question. The life expectancy for the overall U.S. population was a record 76.9 years in 2000. But for today's healthy 50-year-olds, the life expectancy is 82 for women and 78 for men. And once you've reached age 75, the life expectancy is 87 years for women and 85 for men, according to Social Security. Table 3.1 shows the odds that the Society of Actuaries is projecting for today's 65-year-olds. But haven't you always considered yourself to be above average? Why stop thinking that way now? You may live far longer than average.

For a realistic estimate of how long you're likely to live, go to **www.livingto100.com** and use the calculator. You'll be asked to input

Table 3.1   Conditional Probability of Survival at Age 65

To Age	Female	Male
70	93.9%	92.2%
75	85.0	81.3
80	72.3	65.9
85	55.8	45.5
90	34.8	23.7
95	15.6	7.7
100	5.0	1.4

Source: Society of Actuaries RP-2000 Table (with full projection). Reprinted with permission.

everything from medical information (blood pressure, cholesterol) to dietary and exercise habits—down to whether you buckle your seatbelt and floss your teeth. That information, combined with demographic data, may give a surprising result when you click to calculate your life expectancy. (You'll probably start living a healthier lifestyle if you don't like the results!)

Confronting your own mortality is the first, and most difficult, issue in retirement planning. The earlier you start planning for retirement, the better. But you don't start taking the issue seriously until your body betrays you or until your friends begin having health problems and you realize you could be next. Then you see the miracles of modern science and realize that it is possible to cure those ailments and live a longer life than your parents ever dreamed. That's when you start thinking you'd better plan to live longer.

Why bet against the odds? The real issue is whether you'll feel worse if you run out of money because you live longer than you planned, or if you die before you have a chance to spend the money you saved!

WHAT WILL INFLATION DO TO THE VALUE OF MY SAVINGS?

Inflation is another force of nature—economic nature—that's unpredictable in the short term. Just look at the forecasts of economists and see how frequently they miss the mark. Annual inflation has averaged about 3 percent over the past 80 years, but there have been brief periods when inflation was much higher or lower. In the early 1980s, consumer price inflation briefly hit a 13 percent annual rate. In 2002, there were worries that inflation would be replaced by deflation—falling consumer prices.

Obviously, even a little bit of inflation can do a lot of damage. The secret of retirement investing is to make sure your money is earning more than inflation is consuming. But to beat inflation, you'll have to take a little more risk. And that brings us to the next question.

HOW CAN I SAVE ENOUGH?

You probably can't save *enough*—depending on how you define that term—so stop stressing over the dollar amount. Unless you win the lottery or sell shares in your company to the public, it's unlikely that you'll ever have more money than you can spend. Most people can always manage to increase their lifestyle cost to accommodate a rising income. It's a lesson in how wants can easily become needs.

Retirement is simply the reversal of that process. Unless you've saved enough, you'll shed those parts of your lifestyle that are no longer needed, and you'll focus on issues that suddenly become important, such as health and health care. The definition of *enough* will change as you age, and it won't be as painful as you imagine. The true definition of *enough* is a combination of savings, spending, and continued earning that will give you a reasonable retirement lifestyle.

When you're in your peak earnings years, it's hard to deal with the concept of enough because there are so many competing demands for your cash. Just when you pay off the first car, you need a second. Just when you get your home furnished, you face college for your children. Just when your children are in college, you realize you might have to help your parents in their older years. And in the meantime, you have to live.

There are so many important uses for the money you're earning that it's hard to contemplate setting anything aside for savings. In fact, it won't happen, unless you do it automatically—before you see it and spend it. That's the advantage of the company retirement plan or automatic checking withdrawals for an individual retirement account (IRA).

But you've heard that speech before. You know it's pretax money, so you get to save cash that would have gone to the government. You know you might get a matching contribution from your company—free money. That message has been drilled into Americans over the last decade, yet the Employee Benefit Research Institute's latest national retirement confidence survey finds that key attitudes about retirement savings have hardly changed since the first survey in 1991. The survey concludes, "Many workers appear to have optimistic expectations about retirement and retirement income that might lead them to be complacent about their retirement savings needs."

You're not one of them because you took the time to pick up this book. I remember my mother crossing her arms in exasperation when kids raised a fuss: "Enough is enough!" she'd say. I never could define "enough" then, and I can't now. But I always know when I'm getting close.

How Should I Invest the Money I've Saved for Retirement?

If you've managed to save some money for retirement, the most important question you'll face is how to invest it. Your investment decisions will have a big impact on your retirement lifestyle. It's important that you understand your investment choices and the inherent risks involved in each and that you get unbiased, professional advice about allocating your funds among those investments. If you have multiple investments—401(k) plans, IRAs, after-tax savings—you'll need to coordinate them to make sure your overall portfolio is appropriate.

Simply put, you need an investment plan, not a hodgepodge of accounts, funds, and stocks that might once have been appropriate but now need reevaluation. The financial services industry is gearing up to offer that advice, but you need to understand the basics to make sure you get *good* advice.

Start with a trusted adviser, chosen by more than a television commercial or a persuasive phone call. As you'll see in Chapter 7, you can access independent advice from fee-only financial planners. But you can also get excellent financial advice from brokers and salespeople who work on commissions if you know how to analyze their recommendations and if you get references from their successful clients. If you're willing to do a little work, you can find all the advice you need just by using your computer. That's the new trend in financial planning, and many services are being created to fill that void in giving personalized investment advice online.

Do you need to become an expert investor? Absolutely not. But you do need to understand the long-term risk-and-reward characteristics of stocks, bonds, real estate, and alternative investments. That's a must, whether you're using an individual adviser or a technology-based planning service.

HOW MUCH WILL I SPEND TO LIVE IN RETIREMENT?

Living in retirement will cost more than you think. Over the years, many financial planners have developed formulas involving a percentage of preretirement costs, typically around 75 percent to 80 percent, to maintain your lifestyle in retirement. They point out that you will no longer have expenses for commuting, business clothes, and dry cleaning those clothes. You can eat lunch more cheaply at home, and you can take vacations whenever you find a cheap airfare package instead of waiting for your authorized vacation dates.

On the other hand, you'll be spending more on health care and prescription drugs, the segment of the economy in which prices are increasing fastest. Hikes in property taxes and utility rates can increase your cost of living, even in a home where the mortgage is paid off. And the clothes in your closet won't last another 30 years!

The smart thing is to look backward before you look ahead. Don't try to budget. Instead, go back over your checking account for the past year or two, and see where all the money you currently earn has been going. Consider it a reality check on your current lifestyle. (This process is a lot easier if you bank online and track your spending in money management software like Quicken. See Chapter 6 for details.) How much went for housing, utilities, clothing, entertainment? Now, analyze each category, and ask yourself how much you'll really cut your spending in retirement.

If your reality check tells you that you don't want to alter your lifestyle, then all you need is the income to sustain it. It will be there if you start planning before you retire from your full-time job. Otherwise you'll have to consider a life without expensive restaurants, stylish clothes, and generous gifts to your children. The earlier you confront these issues, the more likely you are to achieve your most realistic retirement-lifestyle goals.

How Much Can I Withdraw Each Month without Running Out of Money?

Assuming you've done a reasonable job of saving money for retirement, this is the most critical question you'll ask. And it's the one question that does not lend itself to an easy answer. There are so many variables—the growth of your investments, inflation, and longevity, for example—that it would take a sophisticated computer program to give you a reasonable answer.

Fortunately, the major financial services companies have designed programs to give you that answer—or a range of answers—so you can plan your retirement withdrawals. That's the subject of the next chapter. But first, you must confront a psychological barrier: invading principal.

Your parents probably had a horror of invading their principal, spending their savings instead of just living on the income from investments. They learned that lesson from their parents, the generation that lived through the Depression. Thanks to medical advances, your parents are living far longer than they expected. Because they have lived frugally during their retirement years, they can now dig into their principal (your hoped-for inheritance) to avoid depending on you. Good-bye inheritance.

But we baby boomers are likely to have no choice. We'll be trying to strike a balance between growing our retirement savings so we can withdraw the profits and earnings to live on, and using up our principal at a rate that will allow our savings to last as long as we do. The more money you take out, the less there is to earn interest or investment profits. It's a delicate balance because the most significant factor is unknowable: how long you'll live. And making predictions based on average investment returns or average longevity can be very dangerous.

There a solution—besides a dartboard—to making these predictions. In Chapter 7, I'll introduce you to several inexpensive services that can bring order to your wishful thinking about retirement withdrawals. But first there are other issues to confront.

What's the Biggest Danger to My Retirement Plans?

Here's a clue: It's not a financial crash or another bear market. The big potential sinkhole for your planned retirement is health-care costs—more specifically, the need for long-term care.

The simple laws of supply and demand are bound to result in higher health-care costs as the huge baby boomer generation ages. You don't need a computer to predict that. Eventually, competition might bring prices down, but that hasn't happened yet. You must factor rising health-care costs into your retirement spending scenario.

If Medicare continues to fund expanded services for seniors, you can expect that there will eventually be some rationing of those benefits, whether by age or income. Company-funded retirement health-care benefits are likely to cost more, if they are available at all. Current retirees have learned that those promises don't hold up under the threat of rising costs that sink corporate profits. There's always a loophole in the fine print.

The most devastating cost of living longer won't be the expensive medical or pharmaceutical needs. It will be the cost of long-term custodial care, which is not covered under Medicare, Medicare supplements, or Social Security. State Medicaid programs for the impoverished do cover the cost of long-term care, but mostly in state-financed nursing homes. One visit will tell you that's not where you want to spend your retirement years.

Because government appears to be offering free long-term care under Medicaid, many retirees are being advised to spend down or to transfer their assets so they can qualify for this needs-based program. That's a mistake that will mushroom in consequences as more baby boomers need care. Retirees who don't have private long-term care insurance policies will have few choices. They'll be placed in a

Medicaid-funded nursing facility that will be overwhelmed by the duality of aging boomers and state budget cutbacks. And states will "look back" for many years to recapture assets that were transferred to family members.

It's wise to purchase long-term care insurance coverage while you are young and healthy so you'll have the option of remaining in your home and choosing the type of home health care or assisted-living facility you want. If you start early, it's simple and inexpensive. I'll show you how to avoid this looming crisis in Part Five.

HOW CAN I EARN MONEY DURING RETIREMENT?

Now is the time to start thinking about your ability to earn money during retirement. If you've worked at a job for years, figure out creative ways for the company to keep you on part time. Or use your corporate experience to start a new career as a self-employed consultant. This is the time to do an assessment. Abilities that you take for granted—using a computer, sales or management skills, leadership talents—might be in demand at nonprofit organizations that can pay you a salary. Or you might find fulfillment, as well as money, in teaching your skills to others.

The worst time to confront this issue is the month before you retire, when you're emotional and facing disruption in your everyday life. If you start to volunteer or to build a business on the side while you're still on the job, your transition to part-time work or self-employment will be a lot easier. Of course, you'll have to consider the impact of earnings on other benefits, such as Social Security, which we'll do in Chapter 12.

HOW CAN I RETAIN CONTROL OF MY FINANCIAL LIFE?

Managing your money in retirement is more complicated than it was when you were working full time because you'll have to confront issues that were handled automatically by your employer. The time to set up a system is now, before you retire. The issue is control. You need to track what's coming in, what's going out, what's growing, and what's shrinking. You would never ignore warnings signs of an illness. Similarly, you'll want to be on top of your finances on a daily or weekly basis. Chapter 5 gives you easy ways to gain control of your finances.

When you retire, you may have to file a quarterly tax return to cover the taxes you owe on self-employment or investment income. No longer will a company payroll department deduct taxes automatically, making tax withholding simple. And if you're self-employed, you'll face a different tax table, along with the complexity of multiple earnings sources.

You'll confront the physical issue of managing your retirement accounts, both IRA and 401(k) or 403(b) plans. You may want to roll them into a single account at one financial services company, just to simplify the tracking process and asset allocation decisions. There are online tracking and asset rebalancing programs; but since most firms still send out paper statements, you'll need to set up a filing system or face being buried in a blizzard of paper.

Consolidation will make it easier to deal with your next major hurdle: required minimum distributions from your tax-deferred IRA and 401(k) rollover retirement accounts. You'll need to aggregate the value of all your tax-deferred retirement accounts and choose a formula to determine the dollar amount required to be taken out each year. Then you have to decide which accounts to take the money out of and which investments to liquidate. See Chapter 11 for an explanation of the rules governing required minimum distributions.

But that doesn't end your retirement busywork. Once you start a program of withdrawals, you'll definitely have to stick to some sort of budget. What happens if you overspend? You can take an extra check from that tempting pile of money, but what's the impact down the road? You have to be even more vigilant about money management when there's a finite amount of money and an infinite amount of spare time.

Clearly, you won't be able to throw away your desk and computer once you retire! In fact, those tools become even more valuable in minimizing the time and energy you need to devote to retirement financial issues. Because that's what retirement is supposed to be all about—less stress, not more.

WHAT IF I HAVE MONEY LEFT OVER WHEN I DIE?

Although you might think it unlikely—after reading about rising costs, inflation, and longevity—it's possible that you might be below average, after all. Instead of living to nearly 100, you might be one of those who balance the averages by going on ahead earlier than you expected. Or your investments might catch an updraft and grow faster than you can spend them.

It's wise to have a plan for what's leftover, if only to keep your hard-earned, hard-saved, and dream-filled dollars from going to the government. Instead, you'll want those benefits to go to your family, friends, or the charity of your choice. A simple estate plan based on a revocable living trust is the key ingredient. And even if you don't have a lot of assets, you'll want to have a health-care power of attorney for medical emergencies and a living will, which instructs on your wishes when life support is required.

After all, why go to all the trouble of planning and accumulating for your retirement without taking the final step of contemplating the end result. It's just a question of timing. And I've always believed that timing favors the most prepared. You'll find a simple estate planning checklist in Chapter 18. If your money runs out at the end but you still want to leave cash to your kids, you'll be interested in the life insurance section of that chapter.

GETTING THE ANSWERS

Now that we've talked about the questions you must confront in planning your retirement, what about finding the answers? That's a lot easier than you might think. While managing all these variables can overwhelm the human brain, it's relatively simple for a well-programmed computer. In fact, that is what's behind the next revolution in the financial services industry. Financial companies—ranging from banks to brokerage firms to mutual fund companies to insurers—to individual planners spent the last two decades of the twentieth century focused on gathering assets under management. Now they're ready to help boomers manage and control their growing pool of retirement assets.

Computers will do the difficult work of sorting your individual goals and assets and then prioritizing the retirement scenarios that assure your money will last as long as you do. But it's not all technology. Computer results are only as good as the information you put in and the programs that manage the data. We all want our hands held by a knowledgeable person.

So whether you've saved a bundle and don't know what to do with it or haven't started saving at all, this is the time to face up to the future. It may take major changes in your current lifestyle and some adjustments in your expectations to make your dreams of retirement possible, but there's no reason to despair. The numbers aren't that Savage, after all.

THE IMPACT OF INFLATION ON YOUR SAVINGS

There's a handy mathematical shortcut called the rule of 72. It says that if you divide any number into 72, the resulting answer is the number of years it will take for your money to double—or for its buying power to be cut in half by inflation. For example, if you estimate that inflation will average 3 percent, dividing that number into 72 tells you that in roughly 25 years your buying power will be cut in half. That means you'll need twice the number of today's dollars to buy the same goods and services. Conversely, if you expect to earn 6 percent annually on your money, dividing that number into 72 tells you that your money will double in 12 years.

When planning your retirement, you must take both aspects into consideration—not only how your money will grow, but how your spending power may be diminished!

PART 2

MONTE CARLO YOUR MONEY

CHAPTER 4

THE SAVAGE ANSWER: MONTE CARLO MODELING

o, I'm not suggesting gambling. You want the answer to that key question: How much money will you need in order to retire? The answer is simple. All you have to do is factor in your current assets, how much they will grow in value over your life expectancy, and how much they will be devalued by inflation. Then decide how much income you'll need to maintain your lifestyle over the rest of your life. The sophisticated computer program that deals with all these variables is called *Monte Carlo modeling.*

MONTE CARLO MODELING— HOW IT WORKS

Despite the name, Monte Carlo modeling has nothing to do with gambling. It's simply the statistical science of modeling multiple alternatives to come up with a likely range of probable results. Monte Carlo was a code name for a technique employed during the Manhattan Project to create the atom bomb. Now it is being used to describe this simulation process, which has been made easier, faster, and more accessible by today's computers.

Stanford University professor and noted Monte Carlo modeling

expert Dr. Sam Savage (no relation) explains the advantages of Monte Carlo modeling over the use of averages by telling the story of the man who drowned crossing a river that had an average depth of just three feet. Unfortunately, that average depth masked the fact that the water was ankle deep near the banks and nine feet deep in the center. On average, he would have crossed the river easily; in reality, he drowned!

Dr. Savage calls it the "flaw of averages," a fallacy he says is as fundamental as the old belief that the earth is flat. He notes that when faced with an uncertainty such as future sales, interest rates, or investment returns, many people succumb to the temptation of replacing the uncertain number with a single average value. Roughly translated, the flaw of averages states: *Plans based on average assumptions will be wrong on average.*

Monte Carlo modeling goes far beyond the law of averages. It's useful because in practice there is no one average number that is sufficient for making good investment decisions. The beauty of

Monte Carlo is that it illustrates the range of probabilities so that you can observe the trade-off between risk and return. In fact, if you make forecasts and take action based only on the average results, you're making a big mistake.

BEWARE OF AVERAGES

If it were just a matter of simple math, you could create a plan that would look like the chart in Table 4.1. On the left is the income you might need (add 000 for thousands), and across the top is the compound rate of return you might hope to gain from your investments. So if you need $20,000 a year in income and you expect to earn 6 percent annually, you will need $319,000 in an investment that continues to compound at that rate. (Zero coupon bond funds perform the job of compounding your money.)

But it's not so simple. This table uses averages, but none of us lives in the average. Sometimes there are ups, and sometimes there are downs. So unless you're using a computer program especially designed to look at all those probabilities—everything from the variability of investment returns of various asset classes to the likelihood of different levels of inflation—a simple chart with average returns is very misleading.

If you want a picture of how dangerous the use of averages can be when it comes to financial planning, consider the story of Joe,

Table 4.1 Assets Needed to Generate 40 Years of Income (dollar amounts in 000s)

	Rate of Return			
Income	2%	4%	6%	8%
$ 15	$ 419	$ 309	$ 239	$ 193
20	558	412	319	258
25	698	515	399	322
35	977	720	558	451
50	1,395	1,029	797	644
75	2,093	1,544	1,196	966
100	2,790	2,058	1,595	1,288

who retired in 1969. When he reached the age of 65 back in 1969, Joe went to a retirement planner with his $250,000 in savings. The planner advised a conservative allocation: 60 percent stocks, 30 percent bonds, and 10 percent cash or money market accounts, as shown in Figure 4.1.

Based on historical averages, the planner told Joe he might expect an average annual return on his investments of between 10 percent and 12 percent over the next 30 years. In hindsight—which we have, since Joe's portfolio was created in 1969—we see in Figure 4.2 that his portfolio did indeed have an average annual return of 11.7 percent over that 30-year period.

Back in 1969, the retirement planner told Joe that based on his forecast of an average annual return of between 10 percent and 12 percent, he could take out 8.5 percent of his principal every year to live on. Under that scenario, depicted in Figure 4.3, Joe would not run out of money for 30 years, at which time he would be 95. The planner noted that if Joe were still alive at that age, he probably wouldn't notice that he had run out of money!

But that forecast was based on averages, and the period between 1969 and 1999 was a period of extremes. The Dow Jones Industrial Average, which was below 800 in the early 1970s, stayed around that low level until 1982 before taking off on an incredible bull run that took it over 10,000. The average annual return for stocks (including dividends) in that period was nearly 12 percent. If Joe had started withdrawing his 8.5 percent cash in those early bear market years, as shown in Figure 4.4, his account would have been so depleted that he would have run out of money in just 11 years (by 1981)—before the bull market even began.

The moral of this story: Beware of averages!

MONTE CARLO MODELING AND RETIREMENT PLANNING

Obviously, you can't use simple averages to make investment decisions for your retirement security. Average investment returns are just one component of the picture. You'll also want to know how those averages were created. For example, how long was the period

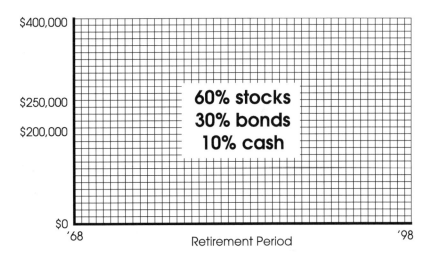

Figure 4.1   Joe's Retirement Portfolio in 1969
Source: T. Rowe Price Associates, Inc. Reprinted with permission.

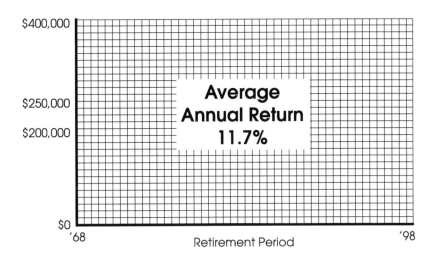

Figure 4.2   Portfolio's Average Return, 1969–1999
Source: T. Rowe Price Associates, Inc. Reprinted with permission.

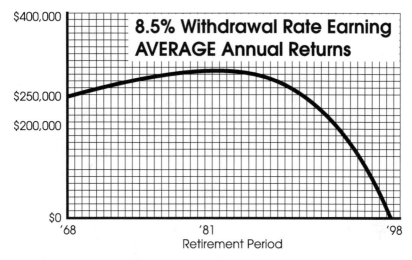

Figure 4.3   Planner's Withdrawal Advice
Source: T. Rowe Price Associates, Inc. Reprinted with permission.

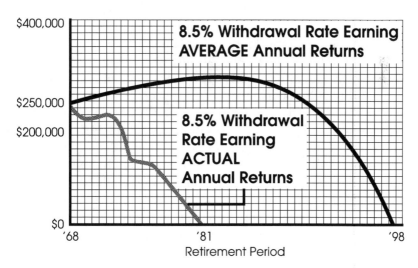

Figure 4.4   What Really Happened: Joe Ran Out of Money in 11 Years
Source: T. Rowe Price Associates, Inc. Reprinted with permission.

of time used to compute the average return? You'll want to know the range of extremes from that average midpoint. Statisticians call it the *standard deviation,* but it's helpful just to think of it as the "range of highs and lows."

These days it is much easier to take advantage of the benefits of Monte Carlo simulations for investment and retirement planning. These tools are becoming widely available at many financial services firms. They create an incentive for employees to bring their assets together for analysis on reaching retirement goals, and for those approaching retirement to create an investment-and-withdrawal plan that suits their goals and lifestyle.

The basis of Monte Carlo financial planning is to take all those variables related to investment returns, inflation, and income goals and evaluate the range of possible outcomes when these variables are matched in different ways. It's the kind of analysis that requires a sophisticated computer program and a great deal of information. Some of that information is easily available

We know about the historic performance of stocks and categories of stocks such as large capitalization and small companies. Computers can also track returns on various types of bonds. There is historical data about the range of interest rates and inflation numbers. The Monte Carlo computer models run thousands of simulations to see how a strategy plays out over all the various combinations.

Figure 4.5 shows the results of Monte Carlo simulations modeling the probability of maintaining a retirement spending strategy over a period of 30 years, withdrawing only 4 percent of your assets the first year and increasing that amount by 3 percent for inflation each year.

Your assets can be invested in various combinations of stocks, bonds, and cash. Looking at the bottom line, you'll see that if you invested 100 percent of your money in bonds, you would have a 91 percent chance of not running out of money over your lifetime. Yes, bonds are safe and secure, but as you get to the date when you sell your last shares of your diversified bond fund, there is still a very small possibility that interest rates will be at a level where your portfolio might be devalued by enough so that you don't have a complete certainty of not running out of money. The modeling shows

- Chart depicts the success rate for various stock, bond, and cash allocations, given a 4% withdrawal rate of 30 years.
- To determine the asset allocation for a success rate shown in the chart:
  — Read the left-hand axis for the percent allocation to equities.
  — Read the bottom axis for the percent allocation to bonds.
  — Any remaining allocation is the percent invested in cash.

Example: A 40% equity and 60% fixed income allocation had a 94% success rate.

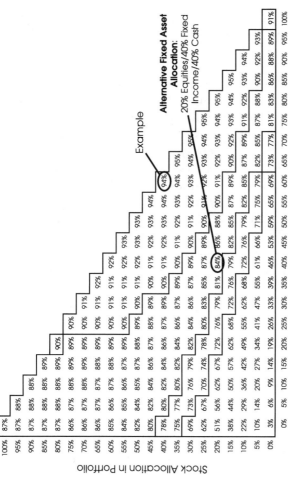

Example

Alternative Fixed Asset Allocation:
20% Equities/40% Fixed Income/40% Cash

Stock Allocation in Portfolio

Note: 5,000 Monte Carlo simulations. The underlying long-term return assumptions are 10% for stock, 6.5% for intermediate-term bonds, and 4% for cash. These results are not predictions but should be viewed as reasonable estimates.

Figure 4.5   Success Rates: 4% Withdrawal Rate/30-Year Retirement Horizon
Source: T. Rowe Price Associates, Inc. Reprinted with permission.

that there were a few periods when you would not have earned enough on your bond portfolio to sustain the payments. But that's a slim chance, based on a broad range of modeling history. There's an even larger chance that you, or you and your spouse, won't live the full 30 years.

Table 4.2 shows a broader range of withdrawal and investment probabilities, also based on Monte Carlo modeling. The table is broken into three segments representing withdrawal periods of 20, 25, and 30 years. Within each segment, you have a range of investment opportunities—a balance between stocks and bonds. (Figure 4.5 has a cash component, but Table 4.2 does not; so the success percentages in the two graphics vary slightly.)

As you can see from Table 4.2, if you are willing to withdraw only 4 percent per year (and a similar amount each year adjusted for inflation), you can pick almost any investment scenario and probably not run out of money over any withdrawal period. But can you live on those smaller withdrawals, or do you need more?

Withdrawing a larger percentage has a major impact on the probability of sustaining income streams over your projected lifetime. That's one of the trade-offs you have to make, and that's where you may need guidance beyond the perspective the numbers give. Most financial services firms that offer Monte Carlo modeling also provide advisers to help you decide on a suitable investment and withdrawal strategy.

MONTE CARLO AND YOU

What varies most in Monte Carlo modeling is *your* input—your personal information and goals, dreams and fears. After all, these programs can't offer a personal retirement scenario without taking into account your own goals, risk tolerance, and priorities. So whether you go through the planning process with a financial planner or a large mutual fund company, you're going to be asked some tough questions. For example, you might be asked to decide what's more important: having a check for $5,000 a month or not running out of

Table 4.2   How Much Can You Spend in Retirement?

The table shows the estimated probability of maintaining several spending or with-drawal rates throughout retirement, depending on the investor's asset allocation and time horizon. The analysis assumes pretax withdrawals from tax-deferred assets and can be applied for any size retirement portfolio.

Initial Withdrawal Amount	Stock/Bond Mix*			
	80/20	60/40	40/60	20/80
	20-YEAR RETIREMENT PERIOD			
	Simulation Success Rate			
7%	56%	52%	44%	26%
6	74	75	75	71
5	89	92	95	97
4	97	99	99	99
	25-YEAR RETIREMENT PERIOD			
	Simulation Success Rate			
7%	39%	30%	17%	4%
6	57	53	44	25
5	77	78	78	73
4	91	94	97	98
	30-YEAR RETIREMENT PERIOD			
	Simulation Success Rate			
7%	28%	19%	7%	1%
6	45	38	24	7
5	65	63	57	40
4	84	87	89	89

*The following asset allocations include short-term bonds: 60/40 includes 60% stocks, 30% bonds, and 10% short-term bonds; 40/60 includes 40% stocks, 40% bonds, and 20% short-term bonds; and 20/80 is comprised of 20% stocks, 50% bonds, and 30% short-term bonds.
Source: T. Rowe Price Associates, Inc. Reprinted with permission.

money for as long as you live. You probably want to choose both, but you have to order your priorities.

Let me give you an idea of how this works. Suppose you're 65, married, ready to retire, and have $1 million in retirement assets. If your top priority is not to run out of money, you could buy an immediate annuity today for the rest of your life that would pay $6,160 a month. Assuming you buy from one of the safest, top-rated insurance companies, your income is secure. You can sleep well, you think.

But wait. What about your spouse, who is the same age? Don't you want that income to cover his or her lifetime as well? In that case, you'll get a smaller monthly check—$5,415 a month—but a promise to pay as long as the surviving spouse lives. Now can you both sleep well?

Not yet. That monthly check might cover your expenses right now; but remember that with an immediate annuity, you're locked into a fixed dollar amount. What if inflation returns with a roar? Even at just 3 percent inflation, your purchasing power will be cut in half in 25 years. Don't you expect to live at least that long? You need the ability to cope with change, ranging from inflation to investment returns. That's where Monte Carlo modeling becomes invaluable.

So while that fixed monthly payment—whether a pension check or an annuity check—gives one kind of security, it doesn't cover *all* your retirement worries. Now let's look at the other extreme.

We know that small-company stocks have a historic average return of nearly 12 percent for the past 80 years. Well, if you invested all your cash in speculative stocks, you might make a lot of money; but you certainly wouldn't trust anyone to invest your retirement savings in that risky manner. If you had to withdraw money during a market decline, your plan would be in deep trouble. Small-company stocks might be suitable for only a small portion of your retirement funds.

The answer to creating a secure retirement plan is to use a combination of investment vehicles: some for growth, some for income, some for diversification, and some for certainty. It is that mix of investment choices and a realistic assessment of how much you can spend that Monte Carlo modeling is designed to provide.

When you seek counseling from a financial services firm that uses Monte Carlo modeling, you'll receive a matrix of investment possibilities and a ranking of the probabilities that you'll reach your financial goals by using each of the possible investment combinations. Those goals might range from a certainty about lifetime income to leaving an estate for your children. The planning process takes into account your other income from pension(s) and Social Security and then determines a withdrawal rate to combine with the investment plan. The combinations give you an overall range of success probabilities. You choose.

Then you have to implement the plan by reallocating your investment assets. And you have to be disciplined about withdrawing money only at the prescribed monthly rate, or all your planning will have been in vain. Self-discipline trumps information when it comes to using your assets wisely in retirement.

So go back over the 10 key questions in Chapter 3—the great uncertainties that exist in planning your financial future. You should feel a lot better knowing that there are solutions available. But first you need to gain some perspective. Are you still in the accumulation phase of retirement planning, or have you moved into the withdrawal phase? The lines are blurred, but you have to know where you are now in order to get where you're going. There will be plenty of help available for you along the road to Monte Carlo – even though many financial services firms have decided to call their products by a different name to avoid the inevitable, but incorrect, association with gambling. For example, Wachovia Securities calls its service "Envision." Brokers at Morgan Stanley call their product "Retirement Design Blueprint." Fidelity calls it "myPlan." But whatever the proprietary name of the planning process, you should ask if it is truly a result of Monte Carlo modeling. In Chapter 7, I'll introduce you to some financial services firms that provide the real thing.

MORE ON MONTE CARLO

For a fascinating and interactive explanation of the statistical science of Monte Carlo modeling, spend some time at Dr. Sam Savage's web site, **www.drsamsavage.com**.

CHAPTER 5

SAVING UP,
DRAWING
DOWN

If you're seeking advice on planning for life in retirement, you're the leading edge of the 76 million baby boomers. You've looked at those 10 retirement questions from Chapter 3, and you know you need help.

But where should you go for help, and whom can you trust to give you the straight answers? Though the entire financial industry is gearing up to offer you services, I have a few suggestions. But first some perspective on two key aspects of the planning process—accumulation and distribution.

During the *accumulation phase*, you're concerned about whether you're saving enough money and whether you're investing appropriately to reach your goals. You might even need help prioritizing those goals. Then, during the *withdrawal phase*, you need to know not only how much money you can take out every month or year, but how the remainder should be invested. Once again, you need to set priorities, either for lifetime income or for an estate.

The two phases are complementary parts of the same project: your retirement. And, as you'll see, there is no fixed moment in time when you make the switch from one to the other. You'll always have investments—assets accumulating—even as you start to withdraw your money for living expenses.

ACCUMULATION PHASE

Decades ago, there was a single goal: retirement. You could pretty well anticipate your retirement date—age 65—and your retirement income—your promised pension plus a monthly check from Social Security. But all that changed about 25 years ago when corporations started switching from defined benefit plans, which offered a fixed monthly check, to defined contribution plans, which required the employee to make contributions to a 401(k) plan.

Since then, the emphasis has been on getting employees to make regular contributions to accumulate retirement assets. Corporations want employees to contribute because the bosses can't put the maximum into their accounts unless lower-paid workers also contribute. And financial services firms want employees to contribute to company plans because the industry provides the mutual fund investments and services inside the company plans. The more money in the plans, the more fees they earn.

Whether you've only saved a few dollars or are well invested in a retirement plan at work, you're in the accumulation phase if you are still contributing. Your company 401(k) retirement plan (or 403(b) savings plan for nonprofits) isn't the only place you could be saving. If you're self-employed or own your own small business, you can set up a Keogh plan, an IRA, a SEP-IRA, or an individual 401(k) plan. These plans differ in their contribution limits and in whether those contributions are made by employee or employer. You can find definitions and instructions for opening these accounts at any major mutual fund or brokerage web site because they also offer the mutual funds and stocks to make your retirement plan grow.

The accumulation phase won't stop until you stop making contributions to your IRA, Keogh, or 401(k), and that may be longer than you think—even past your official retirement date. If you're still working in retirement, you may continue making contributions to grow tax deferred in a company plan or in a Roth IRA—even as you are required to start taking distributions from your previous retirement plans after you reach age 70½. (Remember, there are no

withdrawal requirements for a Roth.) The more money you continue to save, the more you'll have to grow and eventually to live on.

The competition for investors' dollars has resulted in great
opportunities and lots of advice and information for you, the future
retiree. You can see the ads for financial services firms everywhere.
They know you are likely to have retirement investments with more
than one firm, though each would like to have all your assets.

The most hotly contested area of competition for retirement
accumulation dollars is portfolio analysis and advice. The lesson of
the 2000 bear market was that investors had socked money away
in stocks and mutual funds, hoping for a comfortable retirement
based on expectations of huge market gains. Not only did new
investors misunderstand the nature and risks of the stock market,
but they had no idea about important issues like diversification and
asset allocation.

Now the industry focus is on investor education and tools to
make sure those retirement assets will grow in both bull and bear
markets. Those products are expensive and time-consuming to create. So it's likely that the largest and most farsighted investment
firms will create proprietary products, while others will align with
independent providers.

But all will use some form of Monte Carlo modeling to assist
investors in the accumulation phase—whether it's done through
your company 401(k) plan, your bank, brokerage firm, mutual fund
company, or financial planner. They'll help you track your investments, check the allocation among different asset classes, and
model whether your current rate of savings and investment allocations will allow you to reach retirement age with enough assets.

That's the first half of the challenge. Withdrawal is the second.

WITHDRAWAL PHASE

As the 76 million baby boomers approach retirement, the focus has
shifted. Yes, you'll still be urged to contribute more. But now the
industry is ready to target the next great shift for this generation—the
move from accumulation to withdrawal. If building a pool of retire-

ment assets caused anxiety, it will be nothing compared to the worries (and family fights) that will arise when retired boomers try to decide whether they can afford that vacation, new car, or second home.

So withdrawal modeling is the next big use for Monte Carlo simulations. Now that you have a fixed sum in your retirement account, how should it be invested? How much can you take out every month? Where does Social Security fit in? And how much should you continue to earn by working? The trick is to make it come out even—your money *and* your life.

You could take your retirement assets and buy an immediate annuity—a check every month for life, like the old-fashioned pension plans. But do you remember the woes of people living on fixed incomes when inflation soared in the 1970s? They couldn't keep up with rising electricity bills and property taxes. Clearly, you need some exposure to stocks or real estate—assets that tend to keep pace with or increase in value during periods of inflation.

Or we could have *deflation,* a period of very slow economic growth in which prices actually fall, much like Japan saw in the 1990s. If that happened, you'd be thrilled to have locked up 5 percent or 6 percent corporate bonds, while the Fed would have to cut other rates to near zero to stimulate economic growth.

No one has a crystal ball to know whether inflation or deflation is in your future, so financial modeling is designed to create a balance that will get you through all extremes.

THE RIGHT BALANCE

When you look at the accumulation and distribution phases, you might recognize that they are one and the same, two distinct aspects of the same problem. You can't solve one without the other. That's why the sooner you start planning and modeling both your accumulation and distribution phases, the better off you will be.

Before going on to the specifics, I'd like to leave you with this word picture. It's an explanation I've used for many years to explain why I lost my active interest in mathematics somewhere during high school algebra.

The teacher drew a problem on the chalkboard that had to do with a bathtub. The hot water was running in at x. The cold water was running in at y. The tub drain was open, and the water was running out at z. The idea was to solve for all those values so you would know exactly when the tub was filled before it started to run over and so the bath water would be tepid, neither scalding nor frigid. My reaction was: What a waste of time! Why not just put your hand in the water to monitor the temperature and keep your eye on it so you can turn the water off before it runs over? Well, that works in bathtubs, but it didn't work very well with my math teacher. And it doesn't work very well in financial planning, either!

Think of it this way: The water running in is your accumulation phase. The hot and cold are the various choices in your investment mix. The water running out the drain is your withdrawal phase. And what's left at the end of your life is your estate. Do you want to chance your retirement going down the drain? I don't think so. So it's time to get started on your plan. The first step is getting organized.

SEVEN BEST WAYS TO SAVE FOR RETIREMENT

Small contributions can add up to big money over the years. Automatic deductions are best. Remember: If you don't see it, you won't spend it! If your company doesn't have a retirement plan, sign up for automatic deductions with a mutual fund company, bank, or brokerage firm. There is a 10 percent federal penalty for early withdrawal before age 59½ from most retirement plans. And, in most cases, the withdrawals are taxed as ordinary income, with certain exceptions. Following are highlights of how these plans work. Full details are available from financial services providers.

1. **Individual Retirement Account**
   - Limits change yearly ($4,000 in 2007 or $5,000 if over age 50; $5,000 in 2008 or $6,000 if over age 50).
   - Earnings grow tax deferred.

- If you are covered by a company plan, in 2007 you may fully deduct an IRA contribution if income is below $80,000 on a joint return, or $50,000 on a single return. You can make a non-deductible IRA contribution, no matter what your income level. If one spouse is covered by a company plan, the other spouse can fully deduct an IRA contribution if joint income is less than $150,000.
- Nonworking spouses can open plan if filing jointly.
- Distributions are required after age 70½.

2. Roth IRA

- After-tax contribution and tax-free withdrawals.
- Income limits: $99,000 for singles and $156,000 for joint filers in 2007.

Traditional IRAs can be converted to Roth IRAs if income is less than $100,000. Taxes on gains in the IRA must be paid in the year of conversion. But after 2009 there is no income limit for conversions. And if you convert in 2010, you can spread out the taxes owed over two years.

3. 401(k) or 403(b) Retirement Plan

- Pretax salary deduction. Maximum 2007 contribution: $45,000.
- Tax-deferred growth.
- Possible company match ("free" money!).
- Loans are available; but if you leave the company without repaying, the loan becomes a withdrawal, subject to taxes and penalties.

Special Note: Some employers may offer the choice of an after-tax, Roth 401(k) contribution to company savings plans. These Roth 401(k) contributions and subsequent growth will not be subject to federal income taxes on withdrawal. If you are a young worker, currently in a low tax bracket, you'll want to consider the Roth 401(k) option if it is offered in your plan. People with substantial sums contributed on a pre-tax basis, or those expecting substantial pension income, might also want to "tax diversify" and make Roth 401(k) contributions. For 2006, the maximum contribution to an employer's plan is $15,000, or $20,000 if age 50 or older.

4. Profit-Sharing Plan for the Self-Employed (Keogh)
- Contributions are based on income.
- Annual contributions are discretionary.
- Maximum contribution is $45,000 in 2007.
- Account must be established by December 31 of tax year.

5. Tax-Deferred Annuities (see Chapter 13)
- After-tax contributions; tax-deferred growth.
- Early withdrawal penalties and surrender charges.
- Potential high fees and costs.
- First withdrawals are taxed as ordinary income unless you annuitize with a monthly lifetime check.

6. Life Insurance
- Cash value borrowed is not taxed as income.
- Borrowings reduce ultimate insurance coverage.
- Variable policies build cash value, but no guarantees.

7. Your Home
- Builds cash value inside a growing asset.
- Lifetime withdrawals are available through a reverse mortgage after age 62 (see Chapter 14).
- Paying off mortgage eliminates tax deduction for interest.

Note: If you feel your monthly pension check has been miscalculated, contact the National Center for Retirement Benefits, Inc. at www.ncrb.com or 800-666-1000. There is no charge for an investigation. Fee is 20 percent of additional benefit collected.

A final thought: Remember to name a beneficiary for your retirement account. See Chapter 18 for instructions.

CHAPTER 6

GETTING IT ALL TOGETHER

The first step in planning is getting organized. You'll save time and energy if you can present your advisers with your complete financial picture all in one place. It doesn't make any sense to get advice only on your current 401(k) plan if you also have money in previous employers' plans or in an individual retirement account (IRA). Any advice on investing has to be in the context of your total financial picture—including the value of your home, business, and other savings. There are a few simple ways to put this picture together so you can present it to your advisers and track it yourself.

ONLINE, ON PAPER, ON YOUR COMPUTER

You can't reach your goals if you don't know where you stand now. Stick with me because this will take only five minutes. Take out a sheet of paper and list what you owe and what you own. That's the basic framework of a *balance sheet*. For most people, it will be easy to create a balance sheet on one piece of paper. Next is the *cash flow statement*. For that, you'll need your check register and your most recent income tax forms. See, you already have it all, but it's not in a very useful form unless you're willing to take advantage of your computer and some inexpensive financial tracking software.

There are two ways to use your computer to track your personal finances: (1) Keep all your financial information on your own computer and then go out to the Internet to various web sites to update and download your banking and investment information. You can safely store all this information in a password-protected program on your computer, remembering to back up the data on a disk. (2) View your financial information on your financial institution's web site, securely protected by your personal identification number (PIN). Then, if you are away from home and need to pay a bill, check your credit card balance, or sell a stock, you can access your account safely from any computer.

Here's how to get started.

PAYING BILLS ONLINE

If you haven't started paying all your bills online, you're missing out on one of the best and fastest-growing uses of the Internet. Most banks, savings and loans, and credit unions offer free online bill payment to their good customers, saving you the cost of stamps and printed checks.

If you go to your bank's web site, you will see a button to click to get more information and to sign up for online banking services. Don't be afraid that you'll get lost in cyberspace. Every bank has a toll-free help line where trained professionals can view your accounts and help you with any problems. In fact, help is faster with online banking because the customer service representatives can see everything in your accounts, and so can you—at the same time.

Let's address your concerns about security. You may not realize it, but you are 100 percent guaranteed against fraud in your online bill payment. You'll use your own password and PIN to gain access to the world's most secure money transfer network—one that the banking system uses to transfer trillions of dollars every day. If you've been tricked into revealing your PIN, contact your bank immediately. The bank will change your access code, and you will be completely protected against fraudulent withdrawals.

Your online bill payments are much more secure than paper checks. Just think about how many people handle a paper check, whereas your online transfer is just a series of securely transmitted digits. And your payment is guaranteed to arrive on time if you allow enough lead time. No more late fees for missing deadlines.

You can write an online check to *anyone.* Phone companies and utilities can receive electronic transfers to be credited to your account, but many individuals and small businesses are not set up to receive money that way. So if you want to write a check to your sister in another city, you can issue instructions online, and a paper check will be printed at the bank and mailed to her at no extra cost to you.

We've long anticipated the paperless society; and when it comes to checks, we're well down that road. In fact, the Federal Reserve has closed down several check-processing centers because of the decline in paper check writing. The next new thing will be online bill *presentation.* In fact, it's already starting.

Many large corporations already make it easy for you to visit their company web sites to view and pay your bill. But the next generation in online bill presentation allows almost all of your bills to be sent to *your* bank's web site. They are posted there so you can review the charges and dispute them, if necessary, before paying the bill directly from your bank web site. You can specify the date and the amount to be paid. Some banks will even send you an e-mail reminder that bills have arrived at your web site. Of course, it's all done with complete security.

No more waiting for the bill to arrive in your mailbox or having mail forwarded to you when you're on vacation. Online bill presentation allows you to view and pay bills securely from any computer, even when you're away on vacation. This is where the banking industry is going, and it's moving quickly. So get started today—and think of all the trees we'll be saving when we eliminate paper checks!

How does this new technology of money management help you in retirement planning? Actually, it's a central part of planning how much money you'll need to spend in retirement and of tracking that spending once you are retired. If you start now, you'll have a complete financial record of your cash flow, and you'll be able to pay down debt more easily. You will also be able to accurately assess your future needs.

Organizing Your Online Financial Life

You can pay bills at your bank website from any location or initiate payments from a software program you install on your home computer. That's the flexibility of online bill payment. But for financial planning, I highly recommend a program like Quicken, not only to pay your bills online but also to track your spending and organize your data. Quicken's home page and sample check register are shown in Figures 6.1 and 6.2.

There are two ways to use Quicken: (1) You can pay bills at your bank's web site and then download your check payment information into Quicken. Or (2) you can start the bill-paying process at your home computer and use Quicken to send payment instructions securely to your bank. Either way, you'll now have all your bill payment information organized, stored, and backed up on your home computer. It's a good idea to back up the program on a separate disk every time you use it. It's simple—just a click of your mouse to do it.

Quicken automatically creates a check register, subtracts your balance, and reconciles your account as checks clear. (You can even print out the check register to remind you of the old days of writing paper checks and then rewriting everything in a check register!) But what's most helpful about the electronic check register is that you can assign a category to each of your checks and view your spending by category with a click of your mouse. Or you can click to track your checks by payee. As you download your checking information, you'll also see your ATM (automatic teller machine) and debit card activities, showing the business at which the card was used or the location of the ATM withdrawal. Then you can assign each spending debit to a category. Now you have no excuse for not knowing where all the money went.

There are several versions of Quicken, and they are updated

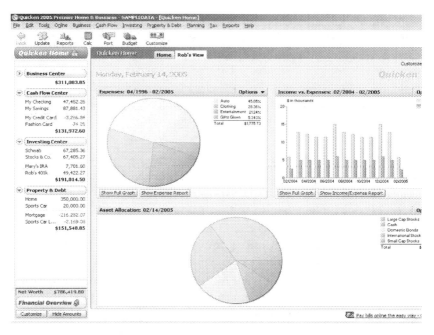

Figure 6.1   Quicken Home Page
Source: Copyright © 2004 Intuit Inc. All rights reserved. Used by permission. Quicken is a registered trademark of Intuit Inc.

every year. Since I have personally used Quicken for years, I'm more familiar with that software, but Microsoft Money offers similar features. Both sell for around $60.

Quicken and Microsoft Money allow you to set budgets and to make projections about paying down debt and building savings for college or other goals. You wouldn't track your cash flow today using an abacus or a slide rule. Similarly, the old-fashioned paper checks and register system can't begin to compete with a debit card and online bill payment.

While online and on-computer programs are great for managing your everyday money, that's just the beginning of what they can do. They help track your investments and do basic planning tasks, such as eliminating debt and planning for college. But to get the most sophisticated, personalized investment advice for reaching your

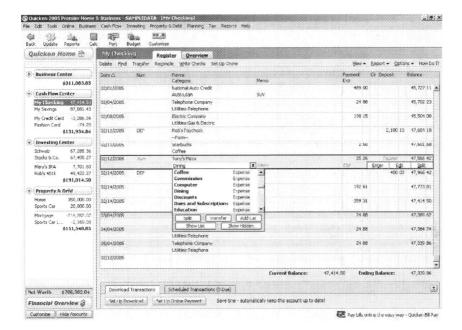

Figure 6.2   Quicken Check Register
Source: Copyright © 2004 Intuit Inc. All rights reserved. Used by permission.
Quicken is a registered trademark of Intuit Inc.

goals, you must turn to secure web sites you can access from any computer.

PORTFOLIO TRACKING

Wealthy people used to visit the bank vaults where they kept their stock certificates in brown accordion folders tied with string. If you had enough stock certificates to fill a moderate-sized folder, you were said to have a "portfolio." Things were simpler back then.

Today, you probably receive either paper or online statements of your holdings from your company retirement plan, brokerage firm, and mutual fund company. That creates the job of opening the envelope, perusing the statement, and filing it in some drawer where you'll accumulate quite a pile. While I'm not advising that you discard your monthly statements, there is a better way to track your investments.

Almost every major web portal offers a free service for investment tracking. They know you'll come back on a regular basis to view your portfolio and update your progress. And in the process, you'll view their ads. Those visits, or "eyeballs," are a major source of advertising revenue for the portals. You'll find PIN-protected portfolio listing services at MSN, AOL, Yahoo!, and Quicken.com. You can track your entire investment portfolio online at mutual fund companies, such as Fidelity, or at web sites, such as Morningstar.com.

Not all tracking services are alike in the ease of inputting your investments or updating security values and prices. Some services exist merely as a convenient place to view and update your holdings, while others take the process a step further by offering tools for analysis and even Monte Carlo modeling and advice.

If you have several accounts at different brokerage firms and mutual fund companies, you can go to each web site to view the latest details. But this is about getting it all together. If you plan to seek retirement-planning help online, you will want to track your investments at the place where you get the best investment and asset allocation advice. The way to start is by understanding your total financial picture before you seek advice on investment strategies.

Quicken

Quicken is both a software package that can manage your finances and a web site where registered users of the most recent versions of the software can securely gather and track information about all their investments—from almost every brokerage firm, bank, mutual fund company, or other investment provider. If you want to do the online bill payment described earlier and the portfolio management explained here, you should probably purchase Quicken Premier.

One of the most practical features of Quicken Premier's portfolio tracking system is its unique One-Step Update. It can easily collect updated information about your investment and retirement accounts, as well as banking and credit card information, from about 2,000 different banks, brokerage firms, and credit card companies, as well as from Fidelity and Hewitt and eight of the largest 401(k) providers. All you have to do is contact each broker or fund accout and set up online access, getting an ID number and a PIN.

It's easy to add a new account and set up the download procedure. As you enter the name of the financial institution, you will see the web site address and toll-free number. So if you don't have an ID number and a PIN, you can get them immediately and start downloading in minutes. You can safely store your PINs for all your accounts in the secure PIN Vault that's part of this software. When you go online to perform a one-step update, you can click on the PIN Vault, and the program will go directly to each web site to access the latest information. No more logging on to several sites and gathering information one account at a time.

The Investing Center in Quicken software gives you access to a tool called Performance Analysis, which lets you see how your portfolio is doing compared to major market benchmark indexes. You can get the average annual return for each of your accounts or over the entire portfolio for the past one, three, or five years. You can sort your accounts between taxable and retirement accounts, or you can view the portfolio as a whole and evaluate whether your asset allocation is on target and see how to rebalance your portfolio. Using data from Morningstar and provided by Quicken, you can compare the funds you own to others in the same category. You can see whether your investment performance is driven by actual portfolio gains or just by additional contributions you've made to your accounts.

Once you've downloaded your portfolio information into Quicken, you can view your entire financial net worth, including the equity in your house, your credit card debt, and the balances in your checking and savings accounts. All of your financial information is securely stored in one place where you can get a complete view of your total financial picture and use some basic tools to make projections for the future.

Now that you've organized your finances on your computer, you're ready for the next level of financial modeling and advice.

Morningstar

Morningstar.com is the outstanding web site for investment information on mutual funds and stocks. A good portion of the information on the site is free, but there is a premium membership that costs $135 a year (or $225 for two years). It's worth it if you want personalized advice and analysis for your investments.

The Portfolio section of Morningstar, shown in Figure 6.3, is an excellent place to organize and track your investment portfolio. While it doesn't yet have the ease of automatic download of information from your brokerage and mutual fund providers, this free service does have some unique and very helpful analytical tools. And as you'll see in Chapter 7, Morningstar is active in the field of Monte Carlo modeling and advice for retirement plan participants.

When you click on the Portfolio tab at Morningstar.com, you'll be asked to create a log-in name and password. Then you can set up one or more portfolios—a secure, password-protected listing of all your stocks, bonds, mutual funds, and savings accounts. If you have already created your portfolio in Quicken, you can easily import all the data into Morningstar.com with a keystroke. Morningstar Portfolio also imports instantly from MSN Money software and from online portfolio trackers at AOL, MSN, Quicken.com, and Yahoo!

You can create a watch-list portfolio just to track the performance of your holdings. Or you can go further and create a transaction portfolio, where you can enter your cost basis to get a better view of your historic performance. In fact, you can create several portfolios, including one for stocks or funds you're just thinking of buying and whose performance you want to see at a glance. You can easily update portfolios by adding new securities or purchases and sales of existing securities. Whenever you log on and enter your password, prices will be updated.

Once you've created your portfolios, the fun begins. You can sign up for a daily e-mail service, letting you know how your portfolio is

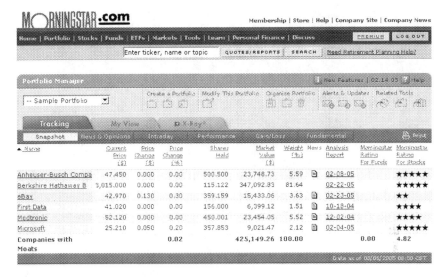

Figure 6.3a   Sample Portfolio
Source: Morningstar, Inc., and Morningstar.com. Reprinted with permission.

performing, along with links to news articles of interest. They'll also send e-mail alerts with at least 40 different triggers. For example, if your security moves up or down 10 percent in one day, has a change in its Morningstar Rating, or has a change in fund manager, you'll be notified.

The most useful feature of the Morningstar portfolio tracker is Portfolio X-Ray. To the get the full benefits of this service, you must be a premium member. (But there is a limited Instant X-Ray feature available to free users of this web site.) Once you've created a portfolio, click on the X-Ray tab, and you'll be given a wealth of information. This feature looks inside your mutual funds to see the investments that each holds. Then all of that information is presented in a series of graphics that let you know how well you're diversified and how your portfolio stacks up against major indexes in terms of sector weightings. You can see the overall tilt of your portfolio—whether to large cap companies or smaller companies, whether toward companies considered growth-style or value-style

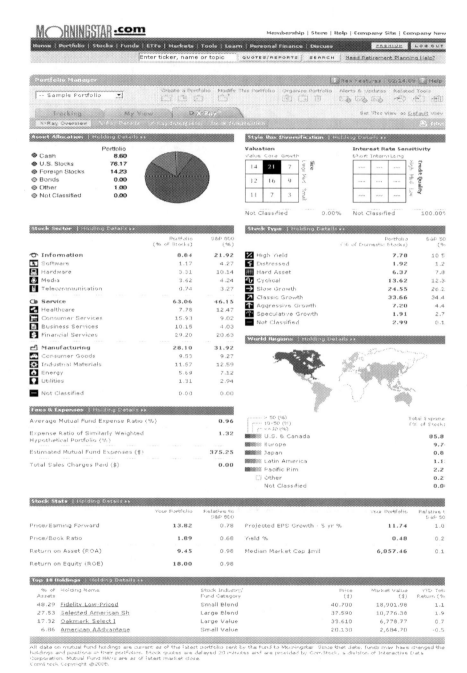

Figure 6.3b   Sample Portfolio X-Ray

Source: Morningstar, Inc., and Morningstar.com. Reprinted with permission.

investments. You even see a report on the fees and expenses you're paying compared to the average mutual fund.

Because Morningstar tracks more than 14,000 different funds and 7,000 stocks, the data is readily available for this analysis. Even though you own several mutual funds and think you're diversified, you'll never be caught in the 2000 trap that saw many funds with different names all concentrated in the same few tech stocks. Using the Portfolio X-Ray tool, you can see how your sectors (consumer goods, health care, financial services, technology, etc.) stack up against the weighting of the Standard & Poor's (S&P) 500 Stock Index.

And, if you've signed up for the premium service of Morningstar .com, you can even see this diversification by individual stock—both inside the funds you own and in the shares you own individually. This is called "stock intersection." Since every major large company fund owns shares in the best-known stocks, you'll see the weightings. For example, your index fund owns about 0.75 percent of its shares in Microsoft, but you probably also have an additional 1 percent or larger exposure through your large cap growth fund. In fact, you'll see the total dollar value of your own portfolio that is invested in each of these companies, though they're inside different mutual funds that you own.

There are other benefits to the premium membership of Morningstar.com, including in-depth analyst reports, stock- and fund-screening tools, asset allocation advice, and a risk analyzer that tells you how much loss you might expect in your portfolio if the market has a downturn. These are all helpful tools, but you don't have to use them to benefit from the free Morningstar portfolio service, which really gets you the total investment picture you need.

Moving beyond Tracking— To Advice

Once you have your financial information organized, it's time to move to the next level—getting good advice. Now, we're going back to the concept of Monte Carlo modeling.

One note before moving on: As I explained at the start of this chapter, there are many competing services that offer to track your investments and personal finances, either online or through software. In keeping with my promise to give you just what you need to know to get started, I've picked some of the best. They are all programs I've used myself. I have never received payment from them, although they have allowed free use of their services and software, as they do for most financial reporters and columnists.

RESOURCES FOR GETTING IT TOGETHER

Personal Finance Software
- Quicken
- Microsoft Money

Portfolio Tracking Web Sites
- Quicken.com
- Morningstar.com

Online Bill Paying
- **yourbankwebsite.com**
- checkfree.com

CHAPTER 7

A ROAD MAP TO MONTE CARLO

At the start of this section, you had an introduction to Monte Carlo modeling—the computer simulations that can generate a range of likely outcomes from a large number of variables. Now it's time to put that great process to work for you, combining technology with financial planning.

Mutual fund management companies, independent online financial advice firms, financial services companies, and financial planners all offer Monte Carlo modeling services. The advice may differ slightly from one service to the other, but here's what they all have in common.

- *Reaching goals.* You may have one significant goal—retirement. Or you may have a series of goals—college for your children, a vacation home, travel plans, or a child's wedding, for example. The best services allow you to model for reaching multiple goals and to see the impact your decisions have on each one.
- *Varying strategies.* The main benefit of Monte Carlo modeling is that it allows you to see instantly what happens when you change the variables. For example, you could decide to take more risk in your investment portfolio, to increase your contributions, or to delay your retirement. Each decision has a different impact on reaching your retirement goal. When you use online simulations, you can see the impact of changing one or more of these variables with just a click of your mouse, so you can make better decisions.

- *Investment allocation.*   If the model knows your goals, it can forecast how a change in the investments within your portfolio will affect your ability to reach those goals. Whether you're limited to the funds offered inside your company retirement plan or can choose from a large universe, the best advice models can direct you to an investment allocation that will give you a good chance to succeed.
- *Withdrawal scenarios.*   Here's where Monte Carlo simulations get interesting and add the most value. Your model will help you create an investment portfolio *and* a withdrawal scenario that last your lifetime.

I'm sure you have one big question about this process: Will all the models provide the same advice if I provide the same input about my age, goals, and retirement savings? The answer is no. Each model might use slightly different data about market history, perhaps because of different time ranges. And each model might run a different number of simulations to create the range of probable outcomes. (The more simulations you run—several thousand at a minimum—the more reliable the projections will be.) And each model might weight the variables in a slightly different formula.

The resulting investment and withdrawal advice could be moderately different, depending on the model used. And since this is a relatively new process, we won't be able to determine which service is best for many years to come. By that time, you will be well into your retirement.

But one thing you can be sure of: No matter which modeling program you choose from those mentioned in this chapter, you'll be far ahead of those who are using guesswork to figure out how much money they need to retire and how they can best withdraw their money to finance their lifestyle.

THE BEST ROUTES

No matter how you do it—whether you work independently with online tools, use online calculators with help from a financial firm, or get all your results and advice from an accredited financial planner—Monte Carlo modeling will be the basis for all the best financial planning. So let's look at a few leading places to get this advice, recognizing that the competition for your retirement dollars is fierce and ever-changing.

Many corporate 401(k) plan providers offer Monte Carlo modeling and advice services to their employees from independent, third-party providers. Companies that offer their plan participants online modeling through any of the services discussed in this chapter solve the problem of data entry; the plan provider does it for you and automatically updates the data for new contributions, dividend payments, and changes to investments within the plan.

Although employer plans can offer third-party assistance for the accumulation phase, they are generally less useful for modeling withdrawals. That's because good withdrawal advice requires more investment options, such as immediate annuities for a portion of your money. In fact, you probably don't want to leave your money in your company 401(k) plan after retirement because you will have a limited choice of investments, many of which are suitable for the accumulation phase rather than the more conservative withdrawal phase. Another reason to roll your company retirement plan into an IRA is because many company plans require an immediate distribution of funds at the death of the participant. That deprives your heirs of the ability to spread out distributions and to delay taxes on withdrawals. (See Chapter 18 on estate planning.) So it is better to roll your company retirement plan into an individual retirement account (IRA) at retirement.

If your employer doesn't provide advice for your retirement investments and planning, you still have several providers from which to choose to get individual access to investment allocation advice. Here are a few you should consider.

Financial Engines

If you're in the accumulation phase, Financial Engines has one of the best modeling services. It's offered directly to plan participants by more than 20 of the Fortune 100 companies and by 100 companies with more than 5,000 plan participants. You can get a one-year free subscription to Financial Engines by going to my website, www.TerrySavage.com, and clicking on the blue box that offers this free trial, which is otherwise unavailable to individuals.

Created by Dr. William Sharpe, the Nobel Prize-winning economist who was honored for his contributions to modern portfolio theory, this web site has consistently offered outstanding visuals combined with sophisticated investment advice. The company is registered as an independent investment adviser because it offers specific buy-and-sell recommendations for your taxable and tax-deferred investments. Those are recommendations for individual funds, not just fund categories. The firm is completely independent and does not get fees or commissions for recommending funds or making trades.

When you sign up, you'll be asked to complete an online questionnaire. You'll need to input specifics, such as your age, current rate of contributions, and the investments you have in your retirement plans. (If your company plan offers Financial Engines, the investment data will be entered automatically.) This process will take a little thinking because you'll also be asked about your goals, including retirement and other objectives.

The computer screens for Financial Engines allow you to move sliders to see the impact of changing variables on your retirement outlook. Your outlook is visualized as a weather forecast that ranges from dark and cloudy to bright and sunny, depending on your financial forecast. (See Figure 7.1.) More specific investment advice regarding switching individual funds is given with the forecast.

Whenever you return to the web site to check your forecast—sunny or partly cloudy—you'll be given advice about rearranging your portfolio. You might want to revisit every quarter or every six months to see how their engine suggests you rebalance your portfolio. If you are using no-load mutual funds, you can easily follow their advice to stay on track to reach your goals.

Since the majority of Financial Engines' subscribers are corporate employees, this program has concentrated on giving advice for

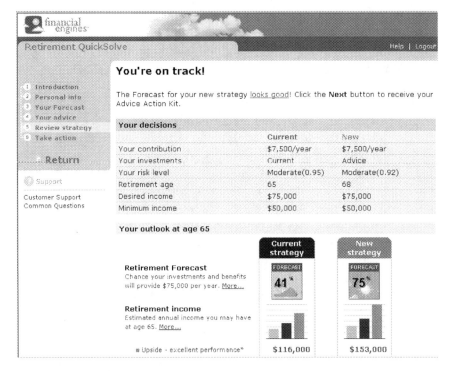

Figure 7.1   FinancialEngines.com Forecast
Source: www.financialengines.com. The simulation pictured is hypothetical and provided for illustrative purposes only. This illustration should not be relied upon as investment advice.

the accumulation phase of retirement planning. It is now creating a model that will offer withdrawal advicee as well.

Morningstar Retirement Manager

Earlier in this section, I recommended Morningstar.com as an excellent place to track your portfolio and to get information on individual mutual funds and stocks. But Morningstar.com's premium membership service, which costs $135 a year, also has advice on retirement planning.

Morningstar bought one of its competitors (mPower) and created an entirely new approach to retirement planning advice, which it offers through retirement plan sponsors, banks, and other financial institutions. It may soon be available to individuals online through its premium service. If you're already tracking your portfolio on Morningstar.com, it's a snap to move that information into Morningstar Retirement Manager. This program on Morningstar .com is easy to use, yet it walks you through some pretty sophisticated thinking to help you establish your goals. It recognizes that retirement might not mean a specific date, but a certain level of assets that will support your lifestyle. It applies the same logic to helping ascertain your risk tolerance, knowing that perception will change depending on the amount of your assets as well as your approaching retirement age.

If you're entering your investment information directly and not from your Morningstar portfolio, you'll have to input all your current investments and add additional contributions to your plan as they are made, unless the service is offered by your employer. It will also model company stock and any outside retirement assets, such as an IRA, as part of its analysis.

Morningstar is adding modeling for withdrawals in retirement. This program will include Social Security and other pension income as part of the forecast and will ultimately include advice on where the money should come from and how the balance of the portfolio should be reallocated. The company plans to begin addressing retiree health-care costs and the use of annuities in the withdrawal modeling scenarios.

T. Rowe Price

T. Rowe Price Advisory Services (**www.troweprice.com**) was one of the earliest entrants into the Monte Carlo modeling arena for withdrawal planning. Although the firm is best known for its top-performing and wide-ranging group of mutual funds, it has long provided individualized investment advice. The latest version of its Monte Carlo modeling tool runs 5,000 iterations, or scenarios, to get a better handle on the range of probabilities for its portfolio recommendations.

T. Rowe Price makes this service available to company retirement plans and to individuals who pay $250 for the initial analysis and annual updates. You can do basic modeling using an online retirement income calculator for free at **www.troweprice.com**. But the focus of their Monte Carlo service is to give individualized planning advice to those who pay for this service. An extensive questionnaire elicits information about risk, priorities, and goals.

Then the computer generates a range of individual investment and withdrawal scenarios, sorted by varying probabilities of success. Each scenario creates individualized investment advice. You get to choose the probable scenario that most fits your risk tolerance. The computer projections are given a human touch by an individual adviser who works directly with each client to explain the range of investment scenarios generated by the computer.

T. Rowe Price views the accumulation phase and the withdrawal phase as integrated parts of the advice process. Throughout the process, advisers focus not on a magic number or dollar amount necessary for a satisfactory retirement, but on a percentage of your current salary adjusted for inflation. As the programmers explain, there is not just one number but a range of numbers and balances that must be readjusted on at least an annual basis. That's what their service provides.

Fidelity

Fidelity Investments has perhaps the most ambitious retirement planning service. It's far grander in scope than just Monte Carlo investment and retirement income planning. In an effort to capture the assets of America's baby boomers, Fidelity has decided it will provide an all-encompassing service for this generation.

The Fidelity Retirement Income Advantage program provides the framework for planning, investing, withdrawing, and reassessing all your retirement assets, from Social Security and pension checks to IRA rollover assets and other savings, whether invested with Fidelity or elsewhere. The starting point is a Monte Carlo planning tool that guides individuals to deal with risks ranging from inflation and rising health-care costs to investment risk and concerns about outliving assets. Then, using your individual input, it will generate both investment and withdrawal scenarios.

The investment strategies model both taxable and tax-deferred accounts. The resulting recommendations take advantage of a broad array of Fidelity managed funds, ranging from money markets to equity and bond funds to annuities. And with $50,000 or more to invest outside a company plan, Fidelity will actually manage your mutual fund portfolio for a small annual fee.

The withdrawal income planner guides the individual through the risks I mentioned earlier in the book—outliving assets, inflation, investment risk, and the rising cost of health care—and creates a sustainable model of regular withdrawals. You can do all the work online by following the steps of the computerized program, which offers explanations along the way to help you make intelligent choices as you input data. A Fidelity representative is also available to guide you through the process, either by phone or in person at the growing number of Fidelity offices.

Recognizing that baby boomers want consistent attention and advice, Fidelity takes retirement modeling one step further. Once the plan is created, it can be tracked online not only to view investment returns, but also to see whether you're withdrawing too much money based on your plan (see Figure 7.2). You can sign up for e-mail or telephone alerts if you're deviating from the plan you've created with your Fidelity adviser. Each year, you'll get a reminder to review your plan in person or by phone.

Fidelity advisers will help you determine required minimum withdrawals from IRAs and will suggest which accounts should be drawn down first, even from non-Fidelity accounts such as bank IRAs. With Fidelity's online bill payment service, you can have pension and Social Security checks deposited directly to your account. You can pay your bills from that account or send yourself a planned monthly distribution from your retirement funds.

This service is offered free to retirement plan participants who use Fidelity funds services and to Fidelity customers, even though their retirement assets may be held in a company plan that does not use Fidelity services. Many registered financial planners will have access to this service while they work with you on a more personal basis.

Vanguard

The Vanguard Group, which manages some of the largest funds and specializes in index funds, has provided a type of Monte Carlo modeling to its clients for many years. Its web site—**www.vanguard.com**—

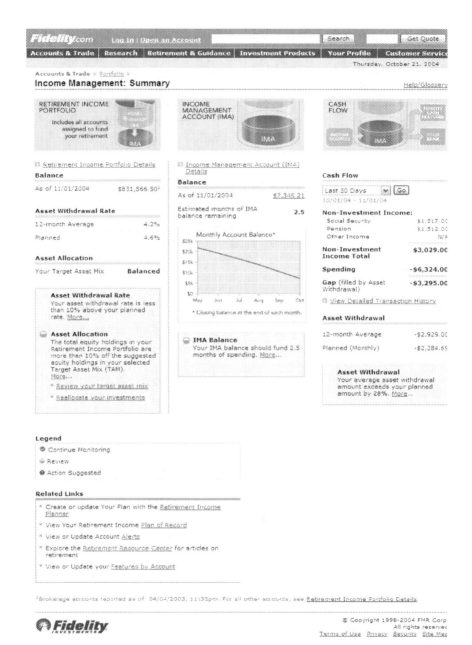

Figure 7.2   Retirement Income Advantage Income Management Summary
Source: Copyright © 1998–2004 FMR Corp. Reprinted with permission. All rights reserved.

has an online retirement accumulation calculator powered by Financial Engines.

Vanguard also offers a more personalized service to clients. It uses a variation of Monte Carlo modeling called "time pathing" to generate a range of probable scenarios. That strategy orders returns from every 20- or 30-year period for every asset class under consideration; then it calculates the likely probability of running out of money for various investment and withdrawal scenarios. You choose the scenario with the probability that lets you sleep.

The fee for this service at Vanguard ranges from free to $1,500, depending on the size of the account. The fee covers a one-time consultation with a certified financial planner who will walk you through the choices and help you develop a plan, using both Vanguard and non-Vanguard investments. They also have a complete and ongoing money management service at a higher cost.

Financial Planners

The personalized services that professional financial planners provide will continue to be a critical resource for baby boomers in spite of the tools, advice, and information to be gained online. For many people who are unfamiliar with both finance and technology, there's no substitute for a professional who can deal with both of those issues while giving you the personal reassurance to create a plan and stick with it.

But you want to make sure you're getting advice from someone you can trust. That search starts with a professional organization that trains, tests, and certifies individual planners. Just as you wouldn't go to a physician who was not an M.D. or a surgeon who was not board certified, you should look for the initials CFP—certified financial planner—when considering a financial planner. It's not a perfect guarantee, but it does keep you away from product salespeople who only call themselves financial planners. You can learn more about CFPs from their web site, **www.cfpboard.org**. You will find a search engine there that allows you to check a planner's credentials and disciplinary history or to get a list of CFPs in your area.

Not all planners are compensated in the same way. Many charge an hourly fee for creating and updating a plan plus, they receive commissions on products they sell, such as life insurance or mutual funds. Fee-only financial planners do not accept commissions or compensation of any kind on the products they sell. Fee-only planners are credentialed through the National Association of Personal Financial Advisors (NAPFA), which awards the RFA—registered financial adviser—designation. NAPFA members can be reached at **www.feeonly.org**.

There's a big difference between a product salesperson and a true financial planner. Banks, brokerage firms, and mutual fund management companies have created all kinds of names and titles for their salespeople. It's up to you to ask questions about their registrations, training, experience, references, and compensation; and your questions should elicit an honest response. Trust your instincts. If you have any doubts, walk away. You may not know much about financial planning, but you haven't reached this point in life without learning an awful lot about people.

ARRIVING IN MONTE CARLO

So now you've seen the future of financial planning. Guesswork, estimation, and paper-and-pencil calculations are a thing of the past. There's mystery inside those computer black-box programs, but they're being designed by mathematicians and statisticians. Monte Carlo modeling is simply the process of rolling the dice a huge number of times to see the likelihood of different outcomes. A computer can roll those dice millions of times in just a moment or two and give you results.

Keep in mind that your personal circumstances can change over time. What might be a good plan at age 60 or 65 could be impacted later by a variety of circumstances, including unexpected medical expenses, a death in the family, or even an unexpected increase in your assets from an inheritance. Planning is a process, not an event. You'll want to return to your planning adviser, perhaps annually, to update your data and to consider changes to your plan.

The companies I've mentioned in this chapter are just a recommended few of the many financial services firms that are, or will be, offering Monte Carlo modeling. Soon you'll be seeing all sorts of advertisements for this compelling product. Always choose a reputable and responsible provider. As I noted, there will be slight differences in the scenarios and recommendations provided by the various firms mentioned here. What's really important is that you're doing something statistically significant about planning for your investments and withdrawals during retirement. For sure, your odds of coming out ahead are much greater.

CHOOSING A FINANCIAL ADVISER

Beyond the commercials that give you a vision of a dream retirement on a yacht or an expensive wedding for your daughter, financial services providers compete on multiple levels. Stockbrokers, registered investment advisers (RIAs), and certified financial planners (CFPs) have different credentials and are held to different standards of fiduciary responsibility. And they are compensated differently. Just because someone calls himself an "expert" doesn't mean he or she has the same level of experience or proficiency. You have to do your homework. Here are some resources that will help:

- **www.nasd.com** This is the web site of the National Association of Securities Dealers. Click on BrokerCheck to find a salesperson's background.
- **www.sec.gov** The Securities and Exchange Commission web site has a section called Enforcement, where you can see the names of suspended firms, read about suspected scams, or report an abuse.
- **www.morningstar.com** Click on Fiduciary Grade to evaluate a mutual fund in terms of its shareholder responsibility.
- **www.cfpboard.org** The web site of certified financial planners allows you to search for credentialed planners and to check on their registration and disciplinary history.
- **www.feeonly.org** This is the web site of credentialed financial planners who do not charge commissions on products they sell but work on a fee-only basis.

PART
3

INVESTING
FOR
RETIREMENT

CHAPTER 8

STOCKS, BONDS, AND CHICKEN MONEY

D o you have to become an investment expert in order to make smart retirement decisions? Absolutely not. But you have to know enough to ask the right questions and to judge which investments are appropriate for your situation and your own risk tolerance. There are shelves of books about investing (including three of my own) and a vast array of web sites to give you detailed explanations. But this section is meant to give you realistic expectations—and some easy strategies—for retirement investing.

The balance among different types of investments, such as stocks, bonds, and what I call safe, "chicken" money, will change as you move toward retirement and then into your withdrawal phase. Most people will become more conservative as they age, but you'll always need some investments in stocks because of their potential for growth.

Even within the category of stock market investments, you'll want to have exposure to different sectors of the market. You might use mutual funds to diversify into international stocks or natural resources stocks, for example. And as you move into retirement, your investment choices aren't limited to the funds offered by your company retirement plan if you roll your retirement assets into an individual retirement account (IRA).

Investing is always about creating a balance between risk and reward. To do that, you need perspective. And you may very well choose to have professional advice. But how can you recognize good advice if you know very little about the subject yourself? That's why it's so important for you to understand the basics of investing and to have realistic expectations.

REALISTIC STOCK MARKET EXPECTATIONS

Stocks—or mutual funds that own stocks—will probably be the core of your retirement portfolio. Most companies no longer offer pension plans that will generate a monthly retirement check. Today's workers are given the opportunity to participate in a variety of retirement plans: 401(k) retirement plans; 403(b) plans for non-profits; IRAs, Keogh plans, SEP-IRAs, SIMPLE-IRAs, and self-employed 401(k) plans for small businesses and individuals. All of those retirement plans are built primarily around stock market investments.

There are good reasons for making stocks the core of a retirement investment plan. Stocks make it easy to diversify your investments across sectors of the economy. Stocks are a liquid investment, meaning you can get in and out easily. And stocks are easily valued at the closing price every day, so you don't have to worry about getting an estimated value if you could sell. Finally, stocks have a long-term record of keeping up with, and even surpassing, the effects of inflation.

Stock Market Returns—Then and Now

What kind of returns can you *really* expect from your stock market investments? Just a few years ago, there was a widespread belief that 15 percent or greater annual returns were relatively easy to achieve. After all, that's what investors had come to expect based on their experience in the late 1990s.

For the period between 1982 and 1999, the average total return of the Standard & Poor's (S&P) 500 was an unprecedented 18.7 percent. In fact, the three 20-year periods represented by the last three years of the bull market (1997, 1998, and 1999) were the highest-performing 20-year periods in stock market history. It's no wonder that watching the stock market became the national pastime and rising stock prices sparked dreams of wealth and easy retirement. It's as if everybody had a winning lottery ticket.

Then, in 2000, reality set in with a thud. A bear market wiped out $7.2 trillion in total market value. Even the subsequent rally wasn't able to return those dollars to their original owners. The Dow Jones Industrial Average dropped from a January 13, 2000, high of 11,761 to a low of 7,368 on October 7, 2002. The Vanguard Total Stock Market Index lost 48 percent in that period—almost the same percentage loss as occurred in the bear market of 1973–1974. The NASDAQ declined 76.1 percent in the same period, wiping out more than $5 trillion of investors' assets.

Such an extreme boom-and-bust cycle is bound to cut into investors' confidence. People are wondering what stock market returns to expect for the future. The answer lies somewhere between the extremes of euphoria and despair, and it hinges on your time horizon.

Historic Returns—The Big Picture

First, let's look at the lessons of history. From 1925 through 2004, the S&P 500 stock index had an average total return of 10.4 percent. ("Total return" includes dividends and price gains.) The chart of long-term market returns in Figure 8.1 shows that $1 invested in a diverse portfolio of large company stocks in 1925, with dividends reinvested, gives you that average annual return. There were big ups and downs in the market along the way, and you've lived through some of the most dramatic ones.

That top line on the chart represents the value of $1 invested over the years, but it also represents the U.S. economy. And, taking the long-term perspective, you must be struck by the overall uptrend represented by that line.

Are you willing to bet against that huge uptrend, against the U.S. economy and its future? Think of all those people who swore they'd never buy another share of stock after going through the Depression of the 1930s. What a ride they missed! Similarly, those who were burned in the stock market crash of 1973–1974 would

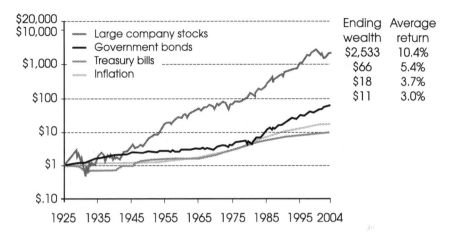

Hypothetical value of $1 invested at year-end 1925. Assumes reinvestment of income and no transaction costs or taxes.

Figure 8.1   Stocks, Bonds, Bills, and Inflation, Year-End 1925–2004
Source: Copyright © 2004 Ibbotson Associates, Inc. Reprinted with permission.

have missed out on the entire 1990s bull market if they had stayed on the sidelines. What future gains will you miss if you're scared out of the stock market by your most recent experience?

It's important to note that the long line represents a *diversified* portfolio of large company stocks, with *dividends reinvested.* The S&P 500 stock index didn't exist back then, but today it would represent that diversified portfolio. If you invest in an S&P 500 index-tracking mutual fund (and almost every major fund company offers one), you could reinvest your dividends very easily.

And don't discount the importance of dividends. During the period of this chart, going back to 1925, dividends have represented 41 percent of the total return of the S&P 500 index. Dividends might not seem important in recent history, as corporate managers used their excess cash to buy back stock so they could push share prices higher and make their stock options more valuable. But the 2003 tax cut, which reduced the maximum tax on dividends from 38.6 percent to 15 percent, made receiving dividends far more attractive. Companies from Microsoft to McDonald's gave more cash back to shareholders in the form of dividends.

Long Term—Do You Have 20 Years?

We can't predict the future for the stock market, but the past should be a good guide if you believe in the future of America. (If you're a pessimist about America's future, then you certainly aren't thinking about retirement!) And based on the past, there's a strong argument for investing a significant portion of your retirement funds in stocks—*if you have at least a 20-year time horizon.*

Figure 8.2 explains why. It takes that top line in Figure 8.1 and breaks it up into time periods. The bar on the far left shows that if you hold stocks for only one year, you have about a 50-50 chance of making or losing money. The bar on the far right is the ultimate argument for stock market investing. *It shows that there has never been a 20-year period—going back to 1926—where you would have lost money on a diversified portfolio of large company stocks with dividends reinvested.* You can pick any 20-year period, even a time during the Depression and

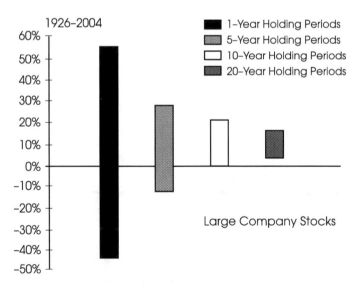

Each bar shows the range of compound annual returns for each asset class over the period 1926–2004.

Figure 8.2   Reduction of Risk over Time
Source: Copyright © 2004 Ibbotson Associates, Inc. Reprinted with permission.

even the time in the 1970s when the market stayed below 800 for almost a decade. No matter what period you choose, you would not have lost money at the end of 20 years, even adjusted for inflation.

This is not to say stocks are the only sound investment for a retirement portfolio. Stocks can be devastating over shorter time periods, as you've seen. You'll need some balance. Alternative investments, such as real estate and commodities, may outperform the stock market from time to time. In fact, they may shine far more than stocks in a period of high inflation. And, of course, some sectors of the market might at times outperform the major indexes.

That acknowledged, if you do plan to live at least another 20 years, these two charts are a powerful argument that you need to have a substantial portion of your retirement fund invested in that diversified portfolio of stocks, while continually monitoring the appropriate proportion of stock market investments as you approach the age at which you'll need to start withdrawing money.

What is your appropriate proportion to be invested in equities? That's a personal question, one that's answered personally by the Monte Carlo retirement modeling described in the Part Two of this book. It's important to know that your model will be different from that of your neighbor, your sister-in-law, or your coworker. And the stock market itself will have its own behavior, regardless of your personal needs. So you need realistic expectations about the market in order to make—and live with—your own investment decisions.

Is It Different This Time?

One thing to be learned from the long-term charts is that every generation had its own fears for the future, its own worries that this time around things were different. That's why you'll appreciate Figure 8.3—a chart Ibbotson Associates created for a column I wrote following the September 11, 2001, terrorist attack. I asked their graphic artists to illustrate the total market returns after several periods in U.S. history when people might have been tempted to simply stop investing for the future. Those were times when America's confidence was so shaken, and the national mood so shocked, that you might have expected major market declines.

The first set of bars represents the three-year period after Pearl

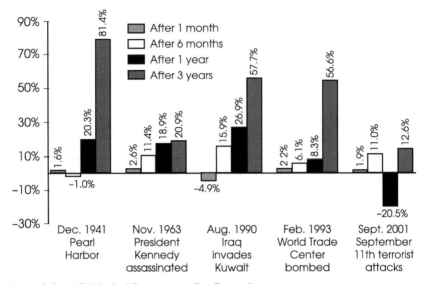

Figure 8.3   U.S. Market Recovery after Tragedy
Source: Copyright © 2001 Ibbotson Associates, Inc. Reprinted with permission.

Harbor was attacked in December 1941. The economy was emerging from the Great Depression, the stock market carried memories of the crash, and the nation was stunned by the attack. Yet three years later, the market posted gains of 81.4 percent.

The next three periods—the three years after President Kennedy was assassinated in 1963, the period after the first Gulf War in 1990, and the period following the 1993 terrorist attack on the World Trade Center—all produced gains in the stock market. The three-year period after September 11, 2001, repeats this pattern. In spite of the anxiety produced by the terrorist attack, the market posted a three-year positive total return of 12.6 percent.

So, as you become a long-term investor, there are likely to be many times when you might ask: *Is it different this time?* It's another way of asking whether you should stop investing in the stock market at a given point because things have changed. They never have before. I believe that as long as our free enterprise system remains intact, the long uptrend will remain intact. It's possible that it will be different in the future, but do you want to bet your retirement on it?

What to Expect—The Next 20 Years

People facing retirement have tough decisions to make. History is interesting, but we live in the present and we plan to retire in the future. Even if you believe in the long-term uptrend of the stock market, every period has its own characteristics that create the overall average. So what can long-term investors reasonably expect from their large company stock funds over the coming 20 years?

This is not a subject for crystal balls or astrologers, although some do try to predict the market using those tools. A serious study by B. Grady Durham, president of Monticello Associates, an asset management consulting firm in Denver, Colorado, gives a useful analysis of the 20-year bull market that ran from 1982 to 2000 and some insights into the future.

Durham points out that the 18.7 percent average annual return of that most recent bull market was almost double the Ibbotson long-term rate of return that goes back more than 80 years. Where did those extraordinary returns come from? Durham breaks it down as shown in Figure 8.4.

Yield refers to the dividend payout, which contributed 3.2 percent per year to the total return. *Earnings growth* is the traditional driver of stock investment returns, and that 6.6 percent is only slightly above the long-term trend line. It's the 8.9 percent a year valuation change that catches your attention.

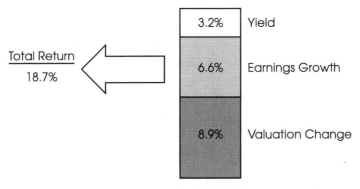

Figure 8.4   Total Return: S&P 500, December 31, 1981 to December 31, 1999
Source: Monticello Associates. Reprinted with permission.

Based on estimated operating earnings for the next 12 months.

Figure 8.5 Stock Market Valuation, P/E ratio of S&P 500, December 31, 1979 to June 30, 2004 (quarterly)
Source: Standard & Poor's. Reprinted with permission.

Valuation change is simply the change in price/earnings (P/E) multiples—the ratio of stock price to company earnings each year. As you can see from Figure 8.5, the stock market has had a wide-ranging P/E ratio. When the bull market began in 1982, stock prices were close to an all-time valuation low, with P/E ratios at 7 times earnings. By the time the bull market ended, valuations had been pushed to nearly 30 times earnings. The long-term average P/E ratio of the S&P 500 stock index is 14.19 percent, according to Ibbotson.

Historically, these valuation changes have neutralized over time, having little long-term impact on stock prices. Instead, the gains in equities have historically been based only on earnings and dividends. That's not what happened between 1982 and 2000. P/E multiples kept expanding, providing upward impetus to stock prices. In other words, the bull market wasn't created by increased earnings or dividends. As Grady Durham's study concluded: "The greatest bull market in U.S. history was purely a price/earnings multiple expansion game."

What does that mean for investors in the future? Going into

2005, the S&P 500 had a P/E valuation of 20 times earnings and a dividend yield of 1.78 percent. Since the long-term average P/E of the S&P 500 is only 14.19, higher multiples give reason to conclude that the stock market is still highly valued in historical terms. With earnings currently projected to grow between 4 percent and 7 percent annually and with a current yield of around 2 percent, it would be logical to expect a stock market total return of between 6 percent and 9 percent over the next decade, at the lower range of historic performance.

Yes, the stock market has defied logic before. But that happened during an unprecedented 20-year period of declining interest rates. Stocks become more valuable as low rates make alternatives less interesting. That explains the expansion of P/E multiples year after year as rates declined. Now, interest rates are unlikely to fall further.

There's one more thing investors might have to contend with in the years ahead: changes in *volatility*. When the market is booming, investors feel more comfortable with high volatility. After all, most of the volatility in a bull market is on the upside. In a period of lower expected returns, high volatility can be downright scary because some of that volatility occurs on the downside, leading to actual losses.

Then there are years of both low volatility and low returns. In those years, investors may actually be bored by the meanderings of a flat market. In fact, 2004 displayed extremely low volatility during most of the year and relatively low returns. That's an important lesson: When the market enters a period of lower expected returns or lower volatility, it requires more discipline to stick to your investment plan.

Maybe it's payback time for all those bull market years. In the next decade or so, stock market return might be at or below the 10.4 percent long-term historical average. That doesn't mean you should give up investing in the stock market. It just means you'll have to adjust your expectations to more modest returns for a while. Knowing the context of market history will help you control your emotions even though you can't control the market.

UNDERSTANDING BONDS

When you're creating an investment portfolio, bonds are often seen as the alternative to stocks. Bonds are debt; stocks are equities. Bonds are viewed as safer, more secure investments because bondholders have a first call on a company's assets in case of bankruptcy.

But on a daily basis, bond prices move up and down, just as stock prices do. You can lose money on bonds even if a company doesn't default on its obligation to repay its debt and interest. Since bond prices fluctuate, if you sell when bond prices are down, you could take a loss. And even if you don't sell, your bonds or bond funds could show a paper loss of value, which you will see when you receive the monthly statement for your retirement account.

How You Can Lose Money in Bonds

There are several reasons bond prices could decline, and they apply to all bonds, including corporate bonds, government bonds, and tax-free municipal bonds issued by cities and states. A multitrillion-dollar bond market trades every day between dealers, even though prices are not posted as prominently as prices on a stock exchange. And, as with stocks, when there is an excess of desire to sell, prices will be pushed lower.

The most obvious reason for price declines in bonds is that the borrower has financial problems. Many bondholders don't want to risk owning bonds through a bankruptcy because there may not be enough assets to pay off principal and interest that is owed to the lenders. As sellers rush to unload those bonds, the price will drop.

Suddenly people are not as worried about the return *on* their principal as they are about the return *of* their principal. No one will pay you $1,000 for your bond if the company's assets are worth only $600 per bond. Eventually, as sellers push bond prices down, speculators may be willing to take the risk of buying, hoping to make a profit by selling when good news helps push prices higher.

Of course, you can prevent the problem of losing money on bonds of risky companies by sticking with highly rated companies that are unlikely to have financial problems. But you could still lose money, even on the bonds of top-rated companies. The reason is called *interest rate risk*, and it applies to bonds issued by even the best, top-rated companies and governments.

Suppose you purchase a 30-year bond from a good company that promises to pay you 6 percent interest every year. A few years later, inflation returns and brings higher interest rates. Other top-rated companies then sell new bonds that carry an 8 percent interest rate. Your old 6 percent bonds are still paying the promised interest, but investors would rather pay $1,000 to get one of the new, higher-interest bonds issued from an equally strong corporation. If you need to sell your bond, perhaps to pay for an unexpected expense, you'll find that its market price has dropped to $800. That price allows the buyer to get an investment return similar to current interest rates.

You don't have to sell your bonds and take a loss, unless you need the cash. If you hold your bonds to maturity, you'll get your principal—the face value of the bond—back. But in the meantime, you might have been stuck with returns that don't even match inflation. It's a scenario that happened to many bond investors in the late 1970s.

The rule is simple: *When interest rates rise, bond prices fall.* The reverse is true as well. When interest rates fall, bond prices rise. When rates dropped to 5 percent, older bonds of similar quality and maturity with interest rate coupons of 9 percent traded at a premium to their $1,000 face value.

How much will your bond price rise or fall as interest rates change? That depends on the length of time until the bond matures. The longer the maturity of the bond, the larger the swing in price will be when interest rates change. It happens to all bonds. And this principle explains how you can lose money in perfectly safe bonds. The greatest mistake is to fool yourself into thinking you can't lose money in bonds or bond funds.

The Advantage of Bond Funds

If you're thinking of investing in bonds, there's another concern to keep in mind. When it comes to buying and selling bonds of individual companies or of states and municipalities, individual investors face many pitfalls. Small orders may not get the best prices when you are buying and may find illiquid markets when it is time to sell.

The huge bond market is not as price transparent as the stock market. That allows dealers to purchase bonds for inventory, then mark up the prices, and sell them to you. You will never know how much money the dealer made on the transaction beyond the commission that shows on your confirmation. There is a web site, **www.investinginbonds.com**, that allows investors to track bond prices on a real-time basis. You can search by name to see recent trade prices of bonds you may want to buy or sell.

For most investors, a better strategy is to buy a bond fund, such as those offered by major mutual fund companies. These are *open-end* bond funds, meaning that the money you invest at any time is used to purchase new bonds for the fund. You can buy funds that specialize in corporate bonds or government bonds or even bonds of international companies or governments. For a small annual fee, a professional manager will choose the bonds and get the best prices.

The typical bond fund sticks to bonds of a specific maturity: long-term (10 to 20 years), intermediate-term (3 to 10 years), and short-term (less than 3 years). Funds that buy debt of even shorter-term maturities, less than one year, are typically called *money market funds.* Funds may also specialize in one type of bond—foreign, municipal, or even a low-rated category called *junk*, or high-yield, bonds.

The portfolio manager of your bond fund has the responsibility of buying and selling the best bonds in the category. But you'll still have interest rate risk, especially if you are invested in a long-term bond fund. Remember: The shorter the maturity of the bond or bonds in a fund, the less price volatility your portfolio will have. When rates rise, bond funds with shorter-term investments will always have some bonds maturing, which provides cash to reinvest at higher yields. Longer-term bond funds will be stuck with low-yielding investments, unless the portfolio manager decides to sell.

Some bond funds are closed-end funds, traded on the New York Stock Exchange (NYSE) or the American Stock Exchange (AMEX). These are just a fixed package of bonds with no portfolio manager.

Municipal bond investment trusts are a kind of closed-end bond fund. Although it's easier to buy and sell these funds, they do carry the same interest rate risk as individual bonds—falling in price as interest rates rise. And prices of these funds may also rise or fall based on investor demand.

Mortgage-Backed Bonds—A Retirement Dream or Nightmare?

Many years ago, the government created several agencies known by their acronyms—Ginnie Mae, Fannie Mae, and Freddie Mac—to help make home ownership affordable to Americans. In that regard, they have been a grand success. They purchase mortgages made by banks and then either hold on to those mortgages or, in recent years, package them up and sell them as securities. Their quasi-governmental backing makes it easier for these agencies to borrow money in the open marketplace at lower rates and then to buy the mortgages from the banks, thus giving the banks money to make even more mortgages. Whether that is still a desirable or necessary function in our modern economy is a subject of much debate. In the meantime, investors have purchased hundreds of millions of dollars worth of these mortgage-backed securities. For purposes of simplicity, here are the benefits and risks of owning them.

Mortgage-backed securities typically offer slightly higher interest rates than U.S. government bonds of similar maturities, which make them very attractive to investors. After all, who wouldn't want an extra percent or two in interest, especially when it is perceived—incorrectly—that these bonds are guaranteed by the U.S. government. Still, mortgage-backed securities do have a higher degree of safety than some other bonds because the stream of interest promised to investors comes from the mortgage payments of individual Americans who hold their homes as their most important investment.

Unless we have a tremendous depression and waves of mortgage foreclosures, you would expect these securities to continue paying the promised interest to investors. But these bonds' interest payments are vulnerable in another way, and it all goes back to the concept of interest rate risk, but with an additional twist.

When interest rates fall, homeowners refinance. As mortgages are paid off, the money is returned to the investors who purchased these securities. A few years ago, an investor might have thought she was holding a security that would give a 9 percent return over the next 15 years or so—until the mortgages were repaid or homeowners moved and refinanced. But with falling interest rates, refinancing accelerated dramatically. Ginnie Mae investors found themselves with cash—and the tough job of reinvesting it in a lower interest rate environment.

And what happens when rates rise? The same thing that happens to other bonds: Prices fall. Homeowners hang on to their mortgages unless they move because the interest rates are so attractive. But those low-rate streams of income are not nearly as attractive to investors in a higher-rate environment, so prices of these securities fall. You'll keep on collecting interest until the mortgages in the package mature. But you may be earning less than your neighbor who waited to buy these bonds until rates moved higher.

Total Return, Total Risk

By now you realize that it's best to buy bonds when interest rates are at their peak for the cycle. Obviously, that's as difficult as buying stocks at their lows. No one knows for sure when those moments have arrived, except in hindsight! If all this is a bit complicated, or even downright scary, here's the point. Investing to get a fixed interest rate can be enticing because the risks aren't obvious. For many years, people touted the safety of bonds for widows, orphans, and retirees. But back then, interest rates didn't move up or down very much. These days, with all the worries about budget deficits, global trade imbalances, currency fluctuations, and trading instruments, interest rates have become just another commodity that is subject to economic fluctuations and market pressures.

Because bond prices can move up and down, you need to understand the concept of *total return* to understand the risk you might be taking when you invest in any type of bond. This risk applies to individual bonds; to bond funds; to bondlike investments such as Ginnie Maes; and to government, municipal, and corporate bonds.

Total return for any given year includes the interest rate you earn, called the *coupon*, plus or minus the price movement of the

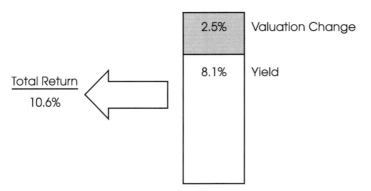

Figure 8.6   Total Returns: Bonds, December 31, 1981 to December 31, 2002
Source: Monticello Associates. Reprinted with permission.

bond. Take a look back at history, and you'll find that from 1926 through 2002, top-rated bonds had an average annual total return of 5.4 percent.

But for the period between 1982 and 2002, shown in Figure 8.6, as interest rates dropped to record lows, the average annual total return of a top-rated bond portfolio soared to 10.6 percent—double the historical total return. This was the most unusual long-term period in bond market history because interest rates came down from double-digit levels in the early 1980s to historic lows in 2002. And, as interest rates declined, bond prices rose.

Those unusually high total annual returns consisted of two factors: First, the actual coupon interest rates were 8.1 percent, a number that the Monticello study says is more than 50 percent greater than the average total return for most of the twentieth century. Add to that a 2.5 percent increase in prices based on falling rates, and you have unprecedented total returns in the bond market.

In fact, those gains persisted so long, and with such little volatility, that today's investors have little understanding of the risk they take in buying bonds: Interest rates could go up, and bond prices could fall. In fact, falling prices could completely offset the interest you earn on the bonds and result in an actual *loss* of capital. Your total return could easily become negative if you own bonds in a rising-interest-rate environment.

Stocks versus Bonds—An Alternative?

You might think that stocks and bonds are the perfect way to balance out the risk in an investment portfolio, but they are not each other's alter ego. Rising interest rates can be bad for stocks because they reflect a higher cost of doing business for a company. And rising interest rates eventually make bonds a more attractive investment than stocks. If you have cash and can get an 8 percent or 10 percent return on a bond, why take the risk of owning stocks?

But history shows that in some periods rising rates are not bad for the stock market, especially when rates do not increase enough to impact business profits or to provide an enticing alternative investment. In fact, if moderate inflation pushes interest rates higher, stocks may actually benefit because this type of environment allows companies to raise prices, thereby increasing their profits and growth. But rising interest rates are *always* bad for bonds because even if rates rise just a little, bond prices will fall. That's why investing is not that simple. If it were, everyone would be a winner. That only happens in the midst of a bubble, like the one we saw in the late 1990s.

KEEP YOUR NEST EGGS SAFE WITH CHICKEN MONEY

"Chicken money" is money you can't afford to lose. It's nothing to be ashamed of. Everyone should have some chicken money set aside for emergencies or just for peace of mind. The percentage of your assets that falls into this safe money category depends on your individual situation.

Having chicken money is partly a function of age: If you're older and not working, you can't replace investment losses. But it's also a function of time horizon: If you need the money within a year or two, you can't afford to take risks with it. And it's partly a function of your personal risk tolerance: You'll need some money put away safely so that you can take appropriate risks in the stock market.

These safe investments are limited to short-term insured bank certificates of deposit (CDs), money market deposit accounts in banks and thrifts, money market mutual funds that buy only short-term government IOUs, Treasury bills from the U.S. government, and even Series I U.S. savings bonds. If you are in a top tax bracket, you might also buy a fund of very-short-term (less than 18 months), top-rated, tax-free municipal bonds for safety and liquidity.

These chicken money investments all have a few things in common:

- They are safe and are generally insured.
- They pay very low interest rates relative to other investments at any time. (If you have to pay taxes on the interest you earn, you may barely break even with inflation.)
- They are very *liquid* investments, meaning that you can get your cash quickly and with minimal penalties for early withdrawal.
- There will be no fluctuation in the value of your principal.

You don't get rich with chicken money investments, but you won't get poor either. You can sleep well with chicken money invest-ments, knowing that you always have access to your full investment.

Chicken Money Investments

The easiest way to invest your money safely is in short-term, federal-ly insured deposits at your bank. If you need access to your money, keep your CDs in maturities of less than three years or use the bank's money market deposit account. You'll want to make sure you're earning the best rates for that maturity. Sometimes banks pay lower rates because there's not a lot of competition for deposits. To check rates in your area (or outside your area if you're willing to wire a substantial deposit), go to **www.bankrate.com**.

To learn more about buying U.S. government Treasury bills (IOUs directly from the government with maturities of one year or less), go to **www.treasurydirect.gov**. You can open an account and buy Treasury bills with as little as a $1,000 investment. The interest you earn is taxable on federal income tax returns but is free from state income taxes.

To buy U.S. savings bonds directly from the government, go to **www.savingsbonds.gov**. Since May 1, 2005, Series EE savings bonds pay a fixed lifetime rate that is set every six months to keep up with the general level of interest rates on five-year Treasury notes. The bonds are sold at a discount—$25 for a $50 face-value bond. The interest builds up over the years. Series EE bonds continue to pay the same fixed rate for the 30-year life of each bond. Series I savings bonds have interest calculated on a slightly different basis. There is a fixed base rate plus a semiannual adjustment based on inflation as determined by the consumer price index (CPI).

No federal income taxes are paid on savings bond interest until you cash in the bonds. Depending on their income, parents may cash savings bonds to pay for college tuition without being subject to any income taxes on the interest. Because of penalties for early withdrawal, you should plan to hold your savings bonds for five years.

To buy a money market mutual fund, go to any major mutual fund company and choose a money market fund that invests in U.S. government and government agency securities. You'll be given a seven-day yield figure—the interest currently being paid—by which to compare funds. Although they are not guaranteed by the government, there has never been a loss of money in money market mutual funds.

Chicken Money and Risk

Keeping most of your money in chicken money investments is definitely not a long-term investment strategy. You can't escape risk in life, no matter how hard you try. Even with these safest investments, you run the risk of losing out to taxes and inflation over the long run.

So use these investments as a safe harbor when you have an immediate need for money or when you are concerned about the risks of other market investments. Or set aside an appropriate portion of your assets to allay your fears of risk while your other investments work harder in appropriate, but riskier, investments.

Never be chicken out of ignorance. Understand risks by asking questions, and take appropriate risks to make your money grow. And always listen to that small voice inside of you that warns you about risks others don't see—or don't bother to explain.

A Minute on Mutual Funds

You can buy individual stocks, bonds, or chicken money investments; or you can hire a professional money manager to do it for you in a mutual fund. By this point, you've heard a lot about mutual funds and how they work, so I won't try to explain the advantages of professional money management and diversification. But I do want to make two important points about mutual funds.

1. Using a mutual fund doesn't absolve you of the responsibility for making investment choices and for monitoring those choices. You need to do some research before you buy a mutual fund. You'll want to know about a fund's investment objective, current investments, and performance record. You will want to know about the annual management fees it charges and how those compare to other similar funds.

   The best place to do this kind of fund research is at Morningstar.com. At this web site you can search for funds, understand their investment style, and compare performance records. Here you can also structure a fund portfolio that will help you diversify your investments. Or, as you'll see in Chapter 10, you can search out funds that will create a balanced portfolio to help you reach your retirement goals.

2. Know the cost of purchasing the fund. Many funds are sold on a no-load, no-commission basis. You contact the fund company directly, through its web site or toll-free phone lines, to request information and an application as well as to have a fund company representative answer your questions. You may also purchase your funds through a financial adviser. In this case, you may pay an up-front (or back-end) fee or commission for the adviser's advice and service. It's always worth paying for good financial advice, but you don't want to overpay. Before you buy a mutual fund, ask about the commissions to the broker and also ask about the ongoing annual fund management fees. Especially in a period of modest investment returns, every penny counts.

These are the basics, but you still need a bit more knowledge. If you're going to manage your own investment portfolio, you'll want to know about different investment tools that can diversify your exposure to risk. We'll discuss those tools in the next chapter.

RESOURCES FOR STOCKS, BONDS, AND CHICKEN MONEY

Although there are unlimited online resources for the individual investor to learn about investing, I always recommend the Learn tab at **www.morningstar.com**. It includes a variety of self-study workshops and online tutorials, as well as reading lists for those just getting started or those with more advanced investment experience.

In addition, I think you'll find these web sites helpful:

For Real-Time Bond Prices
- **www.investinginbonds.com**
- **www.nasdbondinfo.com**

For Chicken Money Investments
- **www.treasurydirect.gov**
- **www.savingsbonds.gov**

CHAPTER

9

BEYOND THE

BASICS

Although stocks and bonds— and the mutual funds that invest in them—are the meat and potatoes of an investment portfolio, they can be pretty bland fare amidst the banquet of investment choices. Some specialty investments, such as real estate investment trusts and gold shares, are useful for diversifying a portfolio. Other less-well-known vehicles can be used to give you leverage or protection or the ability to own sectors of the market. You should know the basic characteristics of exchange-traded funds (ETFs), real estate investment trusts (REITs), gold, options, futures, currencies, and hedge funds. All may have a place in your investment strategy.

EXCHANGE-TRADED FUNDS

You're probably familiar with traditional, open-end mutual funds that allow you to invest more money at any time, with prices determined at the close of the day by valuing the individual securities owned by the fund. ETFs don't work that way. ETFs are fixed baskets of securities that are generally designed to track an index. Like individual stocks, ETFs are traded on major exchanges. You can buy and sell shares in these funds throughout the day, with prices being set by bid and offer, as they are with all listed securities. Depending on demand, the shares in the ETF might be worth more than the securities in the basket, or they might trade at a discount to the underlying value of the securities in the basket.

ETF shares can be bought on margin and even sold short. If the basket of securities represents a major segment of the market, you have a convenient way to own that segment or, if you're hoping to profit from falling prices, to sell it short. Because these are passively managed, fixed portfolios of stocks, expenses within the funds are very low. You will, however, have to pay a commission to buy and sell the shares.

Exchange-traded funds allow a focused, yet diversified, exposure to various market segments in a cost-efficient format. They allow you to invest in targeted sectors of the market or in broad market indexes with one purchase. For example, you could purchase the equivalent of the Standard & Poor's (S&P) 500 Depositary Receipts (SPDRs), popularly known as "Spiders." QQQQ is the symbol for an ETF that represents the NASDAQ 100 index of stocks, which is dominated by the tech sector. Another ETF called "Diamonds" replicates the Dow Jones Industrial Average. The sponsor of that index (iShares) has also created an ETF for major market sectors, from health care to real estate to financial services to natural resources. There are many fixed-income (bond) ETFs, including corporate bonds and Treasuries. There also ETFs that replicate foreign stock and bond indexes.

Because these portfolios of stocks are prepackaged, or created, they typically have a sponsor. For example, Barclays Global Investors sponsors iShares ETFs; Vanguard sponsors Vipers (Vanguard Index of Participation Equity Receipts); and Merrill Lynch sponsors HOLDRs (Holding Company Depositary Receipts), a series of stock sector ETFs. But no matter which company created your ETF, you must buy and sell your shares on the exchange where they are listed.

For tax purposes, ETFs are treated just like other securities. You pay capital gains taxes on the sale of your ETF shares based on your profit or loss and on the length of your holding period, just as you would with any other security. Because these portfolios are fixed, there are rarely capital gains distributions to shareholders unless the manager has to sell a security inside the portfolio, as in the case of a merger.

The low expense of ETFs makes them attractive to long-term investors. But if you're planning to invest a fixed amount every month, you'd probably want to avoid those trading commissions and send your monthly check to a low-cost traditional index fund at a no-load mutual fund company, if there is one that represents the same portfolio.

You can find more information on ETFs on the American Stock Exchange and the New York Stock Exchange web sites. Also consult the resources listed at the end of this chapter.

REAL ESTATE INVESTMENT TRUSTS

Investments in real estate, beyond the family home, should be an important part of a diversified investment portfolio. One of the easiest ways to invest in a diversified portfolio of real estate is through a real estate investment trust. These trusts save the time and expense of buying individual properties. There are more than 180 publicly traded REITs, with nearly $400 billion in market capitalization—the price of the shares multiplied by the number of shares the companies have outstanding.

REITs are simply a form of holding company for real estate properties and services. Typically, equity REITs concentrate ownership in one type of property: apartments, offices, shopping malls, hotels, or even storage units. Other REITs offer mortgages to existing properties. The shares of these publicly traded companies are listed on major exchanges, and dozens of mutual funds invest primarily in the shares of REITs.

The attraction for investors is twofold. First, REITs offer a chance to own a diversified piece of choice properties that could appreciate in value, especially if inflation returns. Second, these companies are required by law to pay out 90 percent of the rents they collect in the form of dividends to shareholders. So REIT shares offer a tempting regular dividend payment that is higher than most other equity investments.

A portion of that dividend may be ordinary income, capital gains, or even return of invested principal. That creates some beneficial tax opportunities as well as a stream of income. (Under the 2003 tax law changes, the ordinary income portion of an REIT dividend does not qualify for the maximum 15 percent tax rate.) This flow of dividends is based on the flow of funds from operations (FFO), which is the traditional measure of REIT earnings.

REITs add balance to a portfolio. The NAREIT Composite REIT Index bested most other well-known stock market benchmarks for a fifth consecutive year in 2004, posting a total return of 30.4 percent. According to statistics from Morningstar, real estate funds led all other categories over the five-year period ending 2004, with an average return of 14.49 percent. In times of inflation, REIT shares may become more valuable, reflecting the increase in value of underlying properties. And in a slowing or deflationary economy, the dividends—secured by rents—make REIT shares attractive.

Of course, there are risks in REITs. If the economy slows dramatically, vacancies may increase, and tenants may be evicted or go bankrupt. Consumer spending may decline, causing problems for REITs that specialize in shopping malls. Business travel may decline, causing problems for hotel REITs. But although income may decline, the REITs still own the properties. That's the attraction of REITs and the mutual funds that specialize in them.

At the National Association of REITs (NAREIT) web site, **www .investinreits.com**, you can get a list of all publicly traded REITs and a quick link to their web sites. You can search by category. There's also a list of mutual funds that specialize in REITs. You can also research REIT funds at Morningstar.com.

GOLD AND NATURAL RESOURCES

Gold and natural resources represent another segment of the investment world that deserves special mention because of its unique characteristics and its tendency to move in the opposite direction from the rest of the market. As you may recall from the discussion of Monte Carlo modeling, it's important to build a balanced portfolio. In simple terms, it's nice to have some stock market winners when everything else is going down. For centuries, gold has been a safe haven in times of trouble and a hedge against inflation. But natural resources stocks and the mutual funds that specialize in them are also in demand during periods of global economic growth.

There are many ways to purchase gold. You can buy bullion bars in small denominations, but they are heavy and expensive to store. You can buy gold coins: either *numismatic* coins, which are valued for their rarity, or *bullion* coins, which are currently minted around the world and valued only for their gold content. A note of caution: Buy only from reputable dealers, take delivery of your coins instead of leaving them with the dealer, and store them in a bank vault.

Perhaps easiest is to buy shares in gold mines. The advantage of owning gold shares when gold prices are rising is twofold: First, shares of gold mining companies typically pay dividends; and second, gold mining shares leverage increases in the price of gold. If a mine is already operating profitably, a higher gold price does not force the company to add new workers or incur other expenses in order to increase profits. As gold prices rise, all the profit drops to the bottom line, making the shares even more attractive.

You can search Morningstar's web site for mutual funds that will give you a diversified portfolio of gold shares, as well as funds that specialize in natural resources, such as oil, gas, timber, and farmland. Beware of penny stock speculations. They abound when gold prices rise. You can diversify your portfolio into precious metals and natural resources without becoming a speculator or a target for scam artists.

OPTIONS

Options on stocks provide a handy way to invest with a small amount of money or to protect the investments you've already made. An option gives you the right to buy a specific number of shares in a company at a specific price for a specific period of time. The option gains in value if the price of the underlying stock rises before the time runs out (expiration).

If you believe a stock will rise, you can buy a *call* option instead of paying for the full 100 shares or paying the 50 percent margin required to buy 100 shares of stock. If you believe the stock will fall, you can buy a *put* option. With a far smaller investment, you get all the benefits of owning the stock, or selling short, but only for a limited amount of time. If you guess right about the direction of the stock but your timing is off, you can lose all the money you spent on the option.

As an investor, you can use options to protect your portfolio. You can sell (write) options on a stock you already own, and you can pocket the amount you are paid. But you have to be ready to give up your stock to the owner of the option during the period of time the option is outstanding. So if you own a stock at $50 and someone pays you $5 for a six-month option and then calls the stock away from you, it is as if you sold the stock at $55, even though the market price may be even higher. You'll have to decide in advance if that's enough profit for you.

Selling options on stocks you own can increase your income in retirement. You can learn more about this strategy of adding income to your portfolio in Chapter 11.

FUTURES

Futures markets exist to allow producers and users of products to hedge against risk. Many of the products traded in these markets are tangible commodities, such as corn, wheat, cattle, coffee, and pork bellies (bacon). But there is also risk in the future value of intangibles, such as interest rates, currencies, stock prices, and the relationships among these vital parts of the financial system. So there are futures contracts to hedge against financial risk as well as commodity risk.

Futures markets exist to transfer that risk, at a price decided on by global market participants. While your mental picture of futures trading might be one of wild shouting and hand waving on a physical trading floor, most futures trading today takes place electronically. But wherever a transaction is made, there are two sides—a buyer and a seller. Only when they come together is a contract made. Thus, it could be said that futures trading is a zero-sum situation: For every side of the contract that wins, there is an opposite side that posts a loss.

Among the futures market participants are users of that commodity, who need to hedge prices for the future. A U.S. manufacturer who is selling products in Europe needs to know what the dollar value of euros will be when he is paid for his product in a few months. And there are speculators, who participate merely to make a profit if they are correct in forecasting the direction of prices.

Since futures are traded with a very small cash margin, there is a lot of leverage to the money invested. Leverage works both ways: You can easily double your money, but you can also lose all of your initial investment, or even more. The major futures exchanges have web sites with educational features to explain how futures work. Check out the Chicago Mercantile Exchange's site at **www.cme.com**.

Although you may never be a speculator, you might want to use futures to hedge against the stocks and mutual funds in your retirement portfolio. If you believe that the market will decline but don't want to sell your stock funds, you could easily sell a futures contract that roughly represents the stocks in your portfolio or buy a put option on a stock futures contract.

If you're interested in commodity futures, you will have to do your homework and deal with a reputable brokerage firm. The first place to start is at the web site of the National Futures Association, **www.nfa.futures.org**. There you can research individual brokers, firms, and money managers that specialize in futures.

Or you may choose to add commodities exposure to your portfolio through an index fund that does not speculate but simply tracks an index of physical commodities. Several funds provide this service: The PIMCO Commodity Real Return Strategy Fund (PCRAX) uses a portfolio of derivatives to simulate the performance of an index.

The Oppenheimer Real Asset Fund (QRAAX) uses the Goldman Sachs commodity index as its benchmark. And the Rogers International Raw Materials Fund, LP, created by global investment guru Jim Rogers, uses a proprietary index to track more than 35 commodities used in global trade. Go to **www.rogersrawmaterials.com** for more information.

THE U.S. DOLLAR

Although most of us will always make financial transactions in dollars, there is a good reason to watch the value of the U.S. dollar against foreign currencies. Amerians purchase billions of dollars of goods and services from foreign countries and pay for them in dollars. The result is a staggering amount of dollars held by foreign central banks. As long as they're willing to hold those dollars and reinvest them in U.S. Treasury bills or other government securities, there's no problem. But if foreigners fear that the Federal Reserve will simply create more dollars—inflation—to pay off our debts, then the central banks can switch to other currencies, although none is as liquid as the dollar.

When global investors sell, the value of the dollar falls relative to other currencies. If you travel in a foreign country or buy a foreign car, you will need more U.S. dollars to purchase those products and services. To hedge your need for foreign currencies or simply to speculate on the value of the dollar, you can use futures contracts traded on the Chicago Mercantile Exchange.

There's another easy way to speculate on the future value of the dollar. At **www.everbank.com**, you can buy certificates of deposit (CDs) that are denominated in a wide variety of foreign currencies and that are insured by the Federal Deposit Insurance Corporation (FDIC). Your dollars are converted to the currency when you purchase the CD. The interest rate is set based on competitive rates in that currency. When the CD matures, you will have earned the promised rate of interest plus or minus changes in the value of the currency if you choose to convert back to dollars.

HEDGE FUNDS

Hedge funds are *not* mutual funds. They are private investment partnerships that operate with relatively little government regulation. With the exception of antifraud standards, they are exempt from Securities and Exchange Commission (SEC) regulation under federal securities laws. And they are not required to disclose information about their holdings and performance to either individual investors or to regulators.

These partnerships are called hedge funds because they use specialized investments to protect against a downturn in the market or even to profit in a downturn. For example, hedge funds may *sell stocks short*—a technique that involves selling shares you don't own, with the aim of repurchasing them at a lower price and booking a profit. Or hedge funds may use derivatives such as put and call options, as well as futures, to profit from declines in stock prices. And they may use *leverage*—buying stocks or futures on margin, thus increasing the amount of profit or loss relative to the capital invested.

There is nearly $1 trillion invested in an estimated 8,350 hedge funds, all using different techniques with varying degrees of success. It's relatively easy to start a hedge fund because hedge funds are not subject to the stringent SEC disclosure requirements that must be met when offering shares in a traditional mutual fund to the investing public. And, unlike traditional mutual funds, where the objective is to get the best performance for the lowest management fees, hedge funds charge investors huge performance fees. The typical arrangement calls for the fund manager to receive as much as 20 percent or more of the fund's profits, but not necessarily to share in the losses.

Some additional warnings apply: Hedge funds are not only opaque but illiquid. You may not be able to withdraw your money until the end of a quarter or even a year. In the interim, you may not be able to get a valuation for your shares. And while there have been some spectacular successes, there have also been astounding and costly hedge fund failures.

Because of the inherent risks in hedge funds, investor participation is usually limited to high-net-worth individuals—those with at least $1 million net worth, exclusive of personal residence. Many pension funds and other institutions invest a portion of their assets in a variety of hedge funds. They can afford to turn over a relatively small portion of their holdings to aggressive, discretionary managers.

To diversify their risk, sophisticated investors may invest in several different hedge funds that use different strategies. Funds might specialize in securities related to merger arbitrage, emerging markets, or the technology sector. They might use market timing techniques, or they might try to remain market neutral, profiting no matter what the direction of the overall market. There are even funds of funds that allow some degree of diversification.

You can learn more about performance of the larger hedge funds at **www.marhedge.com** and at **www.hedgefund.net**. But many of the funds that lose money do not report to these services, or they liquidate the partnerships and obliterate their records. Before becoming enchanted with visions of huge gains, take a cold, hard look at the costs and the risks of investing in a hedge fund.

In fact, that last bit of advice holds true for all the investments mentioned in this chapter. Many of them might be considered more sophisticated, but that does not mean that they are more risky. Indeed, some of these alternatives might be used to actually lower the risk inherent in your investment portfolio. Don't skip over these possibilities, but do research the products—and the people—before you invest your money.

RESOURCES FOR INVESTING

Your broker or financial adviser may suggest some of the strategies or investment alternatives presented in this chapter. Each has a place in a sophisticated portfolio. But never invest blindly. Always do your own research, and don't be afraid to ask questions. Here is a list of resources for alternative investments:

Real Estate Investment Trusts
- www.investinreits.com

Gold, the Dollar, and Natural Resources

- www.morningstar.com
- www.goldstocks.com
- www.dinesletter.com
- www.everbank.com

Options on Stocks

- www.cboe.com
- www.iseoptions.com

Futures

- www.cme.com
- www.nfa.futures.org
- www.cbot.com
- www.nybot.com
- www.comex.com

Exchange-Traded Funds

- www.amex.com
- www.ishares.com
- www.etfconnect.com

Hedge Funds

- www.marhedge.com
- www.hedgefund.net

CHAPTER 10

ONE-STEP
RETIREMENT
INVESTING

Whether you are just starting your career or are rapidly approaching retirement, you may be looking for the easy way out. Aren't we all? I have two suggestions that can simplify your investment program, recognizing that they don't necessarily take the place of professional investment advice. Then there's a third strategy designed for those who think that it's too late to start investing for retirement and that they don't have enough money to get started.

The first strategy simplifies stock market investments. You just buy the "whole market." That's easy these days, since the advent of mutual funds that were designed for this purpose. The second strategy solves the problem of diversifying your retirement investments and reallocating your assets as you approach your retirement date. There are funds that will do the job for you. The third strategy lets you start a diversified investment program with as little as $100 or buy a few shares of individual stocks for just $4.

BUYING THE "WHOLE" MARKET

Instead of hedging your bets through options or investment alternatives, you might want to just buy the whole market. It's really very simple to do. To make the task easier, let's define the whole market as the Standard & Poor's (S&P) 500 Stock Index (although there are many broader indexes, such as the Vanguard Total Stock Market Index, or indexes that replicate sectors of the market, such as the Russell 2000, which represents smaller companies). Here are three different ways to invest in the S&P 500 index, each with different costs, liquidity, and leverage.

Index Mutual Funds

Almost every 401(k) retirement plan has an S&P 500 index fund as one of its choices. And if you're investing on your own, major mutual fund companies such as Vanguard and Fidelity offer index funds on a no-load, no-commission basis. Contact them through their web sites or toll-free numbers.

When buying or selling shares in a no-load index fund, your order will be executed at the day's closing price. So if the market has a big rally or falls late in the day, you can't take advantage of earlier prices. For long-term investors, one day's price fluctuation shouldn't make much difference anyway.

Vanguard prides itself on very low annual costs. Its S&P 500 index fund subtracts just 18 basis points (1 basis point is 1/100 of 1 percent) to cover operating costs. Since index funds don't trade stocks, there are very low transaction costs inside the fund. Major changes occur only when new stocks are added to the index or others are deleted. Otherwise, the fund managers simply purchase more shares of every company in the index as new dollars arrive from investors.

Buying an index fund is the easiest way to own the market, but there are other ways, too.

Exchange-Traded Funds: Spiders

The one drawback to an index fund is that your order is executed at the end of the day. But what if you want to own the stock market right now? Many traders or market timers want to get in and out quickly. They don't want to wait until the end of the day.

As noted in Chapter 9, exchange-traded funds (ETFs) have become a popular way to trade the whole market or smaller sectors of the market. Specifically, the Standard & Poor's Depositary Receipts—SPDRS, or Spiders—are a package of the S&P 500 stocks. This ETF is traded on the American Stock Exchange under the ticker symbol SPY. You can buy just 100 shares or even a smaller amount.

These units are designed as a security with a market value of approximately one-tenth of the value of the underlying index. Thus, if the S&P 500 is trading around 1,140, the SPY would trade at 114. So 100 shares would cost $11,400. If you're buying on margin, you have to put up only 50 percent of the face value.

There are some drawbacks to Spiders. As with any other stock, you pay a commission every time you buy or sell. That cost can be minimized by going through a discount broker. The advantage of Spiders is that you can buy and sell throughout the day, acting on your instinct about where the market is going.

Futures: E-mini S&P 500

There's another, more leveraged way to buy the whole stock market. It's done by trading the E-mini S&P 500 futures contract. These contracts are traded on the Chicago Mercantile Exchange, a publicly traded company where I am a director.

The advantage of using the futures is that you can control a much larger position in the market for a relatively small amount of money. The current value of one E-mini S&P 500 contract is about $56,000. The margin requirement is $4,000, or about 7 percent of the total value of the contract. (To purchase $56,000 worth of Spiders, you would have to put up $28,000.) Of course, leverage works both ways. If the market declines, you can be called to put up more margin money.

The E-mini S&P 500 contract is traded electronically, and the market is open virtually around the clock. It has average daily trading volume of $40 billion, compared to the Spiders, which trade about one-tenth of that market value, or $4.5 billion per day. Individual investors place their orders through a futures broker or through one of the many stock brokerage firms, such as Charles Schwab and Merrill Lynch, that offer trading in futures contracts. Commission costs vary.

Buying the whole market using one of these techniques gives you exposure to equities and diversification within the equity category. It isn't a substitute for an asset-allocation plan that crosses between stocks, bonds, and money market alternatives. For that, the next section gives you one simple strategy for growing your retirement investments.

RETIREMENT INVESTING MADE EASY: TARGETED RETIREMENT FUNDS

Mutual fund companies recognize that investors have a problem: too many mutual funds and too many choices. If you're already intimidated by the world of investments or simply don't have time to sort out the choices, the fund industry has you in mind with its targeted retirement funds. They're a sort of one-stop, no-decision retirement investment opportunity being offered by the best-known and most respected names in mutual fund management: Vanguard, Fidelity, T. Rowe Price, American Century, and others.

You can use the targeted retirement funds for your individual retirement account (IRA), for your rollover IRA, or for after-tax investments that you have set aside for retirement. Some are even found as investment choices in 401(k) plans. These funds allow maximum diversification along with an automatically changing mix of assets that's appropriate to your own targeted retirement date.

How Targeted Retirement Funds Work

The fund company creates a series of targeted retirement funds ranging in five-year increments from 2005 to 2045. All you have to do is pick your expected retirement date and invest in the fund. Inside each fund is a mix of mutual funds run by that company. It's a fund-of-funds concept, meaning that the target series funds invest not in individual stocks but in a variety of well-known stock, bond, and international mutual funds. Other targeted retirement funds use a mix of individual stocks and bonds.

The fund changes its mix of investments to become more conservative as you approach your targeted retirement date. Each fund family also offers a final fund choice as you actually move into retirement—a very conservative portfolio to support withdrawals for your retirement income.

The mix of investments varies from one fund family to another, reflecting disagreement on how much equity exposure is desirable at each age. For instance, the Vanguard fund targeted for those who will retire in 2045 has 90 percent stocks and 10 percent bonds. But for those who retired in 2005, the mix has changed to 35 percent stocks and 65 percent bonds. The T. Rowe Price targeted funds have a more aggressive mix of 55 percent in equities and 45 percent in bonds for those who retired in 2005—a mix that will tilt more toward bonds as the years pass.

Whichever fund family you choose, you will be far ahead of the guesswork that most people employ to build their retirement investments. And once you reach the threshold of retirement, you can employ the Monte Carlo modeling programs offered by these companies to reallocate your investments and to calculate withdrawals that your portfolio will support for your lifetime.

Comparing the Companies

Vanguard Vanguard's program is called the Target Retirement Funds. Vanguard, which is known for its low-cost money management services, uses its own index funds in each series. So, for example, the Vanguard Total Stock Market Index is combined with investments in the Vanguard European Stock Index Fund and the Vanguard Pacific Stock Index Fund for the stock portion of series investment. The well-known Vanguard Total Bond Market Index Fund combines with the Vanguard Inflation-Protected Securities (bond) Fund and the Vanguard Prime Money Market Fund to form the bond portion of each fund. The annual management cost for this series is by far the lowest of any company, ranging from 0.21 to 0.23 percent. The minimum investment for an IRA is $1,000.

Fidelity Fidelity's Freedom Funds, as its targeted retirement series is called, uses well-known funds such as Fidelity Blue Chip Growth Fund, Fidelity Equity-Income Fund, Fidelity Growth and Income

Fund, Fidelity Mid-Cap Stock Fund, and Fidelity OTC Fund, as well as the Fidelity Europe Fund and Fidelity Diversified International. The bond portion consists of a variety of Fidelity-managed bond funds. It is the fund manager's job to alter the mix of these funds within the targeted allocation for exposure to stocks and bonds in each series. The annual management cost ranges from 0.69 percent to 0.96 percent annually and is made up of the underlying fund management fees plus a 0.8 percent overall fee for managing the Freedom Funds. Minimum investment for an IRA is $2,500.

T. Rowe Price   T. Rowe Price Retirement Funds also use well-known equity funds, ranging from the Growth Stock Fund and the Value Fund to the Mid-Cap and Small-Cap stock funds, as well as the International Fund. They also use three of their own highly respected bond funds. The T. Rowe Price Retirement Funds are noticeably more aggressive in using equity funds, even during the years closest to retirement. They say their modeling studies indicate that people facing a 20-year retirement period need at least a 30 percent to 40 percent exposure to equities in order to sustain withdrawals. The mix is actively managed through retirement, and the allocation keeps changing until the equity portion is down to 20 percent after 30 years in retirement. The annual management fee runs from 0.59 percent to 0.89 percent, based on the mix of funds in the series. The minimum investment for an IRA is $1,000.

American Century Investments   American Century offers My Retirement Portfolios with 10-year intervals ranging from 2015 to 2045, plus an income portfolio for retirees. You choose the portfolio that most closely matches your retirement date, and the portfolio manager chooses the appropriate mix of investments in other American Century funds. The funds are rebalanced each year, and the mix grows more conservative as you near your designated retirement age. Annual management fees are less than 1 percent, depending on the fund choice. Minimum investment is $2,500.

If your company retirement plan is managed by one of the fund companies mentioned here, ask to have the targeted retirement funds included among your 401(k) choices. If you've lost money in an IRA rollover account, and don't know what to do about it, switch to one of these plans and let time—and the fund management company—do the work for you.

Starting Small—No Excuses!

Even if you don't have a lot of money to invest, or a lot of time until retirement, there's no excuse for not starting an IRA with a few dollars a month. Most mutual fund companies have minimum investment requirements of around $1,000. Many brokerage firms require significant minimum investments or charge huge commissions on small transactions. Here are two ways around that problem.

U.S. Global Funds—ABC Plan

There is one mutual fund company that has consistently befriended the small investor by offering access to its mutual funds with a starting investment of as little as $100. U.S. Global Investors (**www .usfunds.com**) offers a wide variety of no-load mutual funds that can be purchased using their ABC Plan, which stands for "automatically building capital." If you invest $100 in any of its funds and agree to an automatic monthly withdrawal of at least $30 from your checking or savings account into your mutual fund account, you can get started on this plan. The fund most suitable for growing an IRA is the All-American Equity Fund, which invests in a diversified portfolio of large company stocks. But U.S. Global Investors also has international funds, natural resource funds, and even fixed-income and money market funds that can be purchased using the ABC Plan.

ShareBuilder

If you want to buy individual stocks or exchange-traded funds but have only a small amount to invest, go to **www.sharebuilder.com**. At this online brokerage firm, you can start a regular weekly or monthly investment program for just $4 a transaction, and no minimum balance or investment amount is required. There are several programs, ranging from the $4 single fee to a monthly fee of $12, which gives you six free automatic investments each month. The shares you buy are held in your name or in an IRA (which does incur a $15.95 annual fee, unless you sign up for a premium program). Transactions are executed twice a day, which means you cannot specify price unless you pay an extra fee. But for individual investors with small amounts to invest regularly, this web site is a cost-effective way to accumulate a portfolio.

Remember, time is money. Even a small amount of money, invested regularly over a long period of time, can make a big difference in your retirement lifestyle. Pass this information on to your children or grandchildren, or get them started on an investment program. Now there are no excuses!

MAKE THE CALL

Vanguard Target Retirement Funds
800-VANGUARD
www.vanguard.com

Fidelity Freedom Funds
800-FIDELITY
www.fidelity.com

T. Rowe Price Retirement Funds
800-638-5660
www.troweprice.com

American Century—My Retirement Portfolios
800-345-2021
www.americancentury.com

U.S. Global Funds
888-USFUNDS
www.usfunds.com

ShareBuilder
866-SHRBLDR
www.sharebuilder.com

PART 4

STREAMS OF RETIREMENT INCOME

CHAPTER 11

WHERE WILL THE MONEY COME FROM?

What matters most in retirement is income. Making your money *grow* takes a back seat to making your money *last*. And, unless you are very wealthy and are concentrating on leaving an estate to your children, the concept of making your money last includes drawing down all your assets at a rate that makes them last as long as you do. You don't want to drain your pool of assets too soon, so you'll spend some time replenishing the pool during your early years of retirement. In other words, you may have to keep working.

You may be planning to retire from your job, but statistics say you won't retire from earning some sort of income. In mid-2003, more than 4.5 million seniors 65 and older were working, up 18 percent from 3.85 million in 1999, according to the Bureau of Labor Statistics. Seniors currently make up 13 percent of the workforce, and the bureau predicts that by 2015, 20 percent of all workers will be 55 or older. In a 2002 Gallup poll, 60 percent of baby boomers said they expect to work once they reach retirement age. When asked why, one-third said they will work because they choose to. The other two-thirds of the respondents said they will work during retirement due to financial necessity or to a combination of financial necessity and personal preference.

The respondents who expect to work during retirement are split evenly as to whether they will work in the same career field or choose another. When asked why they would choose a different career field, 44 percent said they want to try something different or something they always dreamed about, 19 percent said they want a less stressful career field, and 10 percent want a career field more closely related to their hobbies and interests.

It seems the concept of retro-retirement—a long work career followed by part-time work and then a relatively short period of idleness—is destined to be the future of the baby boomer generation. The next step is to define just how to balance, and afford, these two opposing concepts of gainful employment and unpaid leisure.

THE BALANCING ACT: INCOME VERSUS PRINCIPAL

It's not just how much money you *have,* but how much money you can *spend* to maintain your lifestyle that counts in retirement. Whether you're staying in the family home, moving to a senior community, or dividing your time between winter and summer residences, it's *income* that turns dreams into reality. It's income that allows you to pay for the lifestyle you've chosen.

There are two ways to approach the concept of income. Very wealthy people can actually live off their income, without touching principal. They'll have a lot remaining to leave to their children or to charity. If that describes your situation, skip to Part Six, Estate Planning.

But most boomer retirees will have to do a careful balancing act between working, earning income on their investments, and drawing down principal at a rate that keeps them from running out of money before they run out of time. So let's examine your possible sources of retirement income.

GAINFUL EMPLOYMENT IN RETIREMENT

It's important to have multiple sources of income in retirement, and odds are that they won't all come from your investments. In fact, the most critical source of income is likely to come from your continued, if part-time, employment. Finding that employment may take some creativity, but it won't be as difficult as some are predicting. When aging boomers are the majority, age discrimination will be less rampant. In fact, older workers are likely to be more in demand as the pool of younger workers shrinks. There is even a web site—**www.seniorjobbank.com**—dedicated to job seekers over 50.

Congress, which has so far been unwilling to deal with critical retirement issues, seems to have faced up to the likelihood that people will continue to work by repealing penalties in the Social Security Act that weighed heavily on seniors who work. Passage of the Senior Citizens' Freedom to Work Act of 2000 repealed penalties on those of full retirement age who earn income while collecting Social Security, even though your benefits may be taxable depending on your total income.

And there have been other changes. The federal Older Workers Benefit Protection Act (U.S. Code 29, § 623 and following) makes it illegal to use an employee's age as a basis for discrimination in benefits and retirement. This act protects people who are at least 40 years old. It tells companies that they cannot reduce health or life insurance benefits for older employees, nor can they stop their pensions from accruing if they work past their normal retirement age. The act also discourages businesses from targeting older workers when cutting staff.

Perhaps of equal importance to preretirees, the Older Workers Benefit Protection Act prohibits employers from forcing employees to take early retirement. The law states that an early retirement plan is legal only if it gives the employee a choice between two options: (1) keeping things as they are or (2) choosing to retire under a plan that makes the employee better off than he or she was previously. This choice must be legitimate, and the employee must be free to reject the offer.

So while everyone is focusing on the possibility of taking early retirement, it's reassuring to know that the law says you'll still have a job, if that job exists. But that leaves the challenge of creating a work scenario that suits your needs and your time commitment. A full-time job may be neither necessary nor appealing.

Your retirement job may not be as an employee of your current company; or if it is, you may be an independent consultant, working flexible hours. Or you may start your own business, using the talents and skills you developed in the workforce. You could purchase a franchise, start a business from scratch, or teach others who want to start their own business. Sales opportunities will abound, especially in the financial services industry, where other boomers are less likely to be impressed by younger, inexperienced salespeople who are the age of their own children.

Now is the time to get creative—*before* you reach retirement age. Starting your own small business on the side while still working at your current job gives you the chance to do a test run on your concept. You still have the fresh contacts in your work life to get the support services you need for your business and to prospect for customers on your own time.

Again, it's attitude that counts. If you look at earning an income during retirement as an opportunity to earn rewards from your experience, interests, talents, and skills, you could have a much more rewarding second career. You know so much more than you did when you started out; you're worth so much more now. And people gravitate to those who have a positive mental attitude. It is the key ingredient in a successful retro-retirement. Even so, attitude is no substitute for income.

WITHDRAWALS FROM RETIREMENT ACCOUNTS

There are three basic sources of retirement income: money from (1) your *after-tax* savings, (2) your *tax-deferred* retirement plan savings, and (3) Social Security—if it still exists in its present form when you are ready to retire.

Those are the pools of money available for income drawdown that will be analyzed in your Monte Carlo modeling of retirement scenarios. Your advisers will look at the entire picture and suggest which accounts to draw down first. Even if you still have enough income so that you don't want to take money out of your retirement accounts (and what a great problem that would be), you're still required to make certain minimum withdrawals, except from Roth IRAs.

Where and When to Withdraw

Aside from the issue of required withdrawals, when you need money to live, you will probably want to spend your after-tax savings first, leaving your tax-deferred accounts more time to grow. After your death, your beneficiaries may be able to continue that tax-deferred growth for a while, making your retirement accounts even more valuable.

On the other hand, under current tax law, your after-tax assets get a step-up in basis when you die. That means that if you have big gains in the value of your stocks, your heirs will inherit them with a new, higher cost basis as of the date of your death. That does not hold true for IRA money, which is subject to ordinary income taxes when your heirs withdraw it.

That's why personalized advice is so important. Depending on your situation, a different priority may be appropriate. But there will come a time, sooner or later, when you'll want to—or be required to—start taking distributions from your retirement plans.

Just don't start withdrawals from your tax-deferred retirement plan until after you reach age 59½, or you'll face a 10 percent federal tax penalty (unless you agree to take equal payments over your full lifetime). And you *must* start withdrawals in the year after you reach age 70½.

Three things to keep in mind:

1. The money you withdraw from your retirement accounts will all come out taxed as ordinary income.
2. You can take as much money out of your tax-deferred retirement funds as you want without penalty once you reach age 59½.
3. You must set money aside to pay the taxes.

Required Minimum Distributions and Required Beginning Date

As noted earlier, for seniors, life gets more complicated, not less, when it comes to finances. The rules for distribution of retirement accounts are among the most complicated. Thank goodness the financial services industry recognizes this and is competing to offer services to help you with distribution decisions.

Here are two key terms:

1. *Required Beginning Date (RBD):* The deadline for the account owner's first RBD is April 1 of the year following the year the account owner reaches age 70½. Generally, it is wise to take the first distribution in the actual year you reach age 70½ to avoid a double distribution the following year, which could increase your tax bracket.

2. *Required Minimum Distribution (RMD):* The amount of the RMD is based on the value of all of the tax-deferred retirement accounts owned by the person, although the distributions can be made from one or more accounts. The amount is calculated based on the Internal Revenue Service's (IRS's) Uniform Lifetime Distribution Table (except in the case of an owner whose spouse is sole beneficiary and is more than 10 years younger than the owner).

Getting It Right

It's important that you calculate your annual distribution correctly. The rules have been simplified in recent years, but mistakes can be costly. If you underwithdraw, you're subject to a penalty of 50 percent of the amount that should have been withdrawn. Your IRA custodian can help you calculate the exact amount of the required minimum distribution each year, using the factor from the IRS table. Just be sure to include *all* your retirement accounts in your calculation.

After you decide how much you *must* withdraw—remembering that you can always withdraw *more*—you then must decide which accounts to draw down first. This is not a matter of guesswork. You should have taken this issue into account as you went through the Monte Carlo modeling process described in Part Two of this book. Still, you might want to revisit the subject every year as you consider rebalancing your accounts. Then you can withdraw more from the sector that has become overweighted because of gains.

There's another issue to consider. Each year, your required withdrawal will be determined by the IRS table based on your age and retirement savings. What if you have investment losses? You might have smaller required withdrawals, or you might recognize that you're dipping into the bottom of the pot. That happened to many people after the last bear market. And that's why you need an overall plan, using Monte Carlo modeling, that covers both investments and withdrawals—a plan that should be updated every year.

As you consider consolidating all your IRAs, Keogh plans, and rollover accounts, this issue of modeling investments and calculating distributions should be a major consideration in your choice of retirement plan custodians. Life is complicated enough without agonizing over the proper withdrawal amount each year. Make it simple by using a financial institution that specializes in these services.

While we're on the subject of IRA withdrawals, please make sure you've named the appropriate beneficiary for any IRA assets that remain after your death. Your choice could make a huge difference in the future growth of that tax-deferred account. Details are in Chapter 18, Estate Planning.

GENERATING INCOME FROM YOUR PORTFOLIO

Most of your retirement income will come from retirement plan distributions and from ongoing earnings. But you will also want to reevaluate your investment portfolio to see if it can generate more income. Here are two concepts that can help you develop a regular stream of income from your portfolio.

In Chapter 9, I explained income-producing investments, including bonds, real estate investment trusts, preferred stocks, and the mutual funds that specialize in these asset classes. You can generate more income by giving these products greater weight in your portfolio. There are other strategies you can use to build income that will arrive on a regular basis.

Laddering: A Bond Strategy for Retirement

In stocks, you can buy a fixed dollar amount of mutual fund shares every month or quarter. You'll never pick tops or bottoms that way, but you will spread out your purchases and get the average price.

There's a similar strategy for bonds. It's called laddering, and it simply means that you stagger your maturities so that an old bond is always maturing and the cash can be reinvested at the current higher or lower yield. You'll never get the top rate for all your bond portfolio with this strategy, but you won't make the mistake of locking up all your money at low rates.

Laddering solves another problem. When you're retired, you want to count on both the income and the principal from your bonds. Yes, you'll hope to live off the interest income, but at some point you might need to sell some of your bonds because you need cash. It would be nice if that didn't happen in a period of rising interest rates, when bond prices are falling.

You can ladder a portfolio by buying short-term securities such as U.S. Treasury bills and staggering your purchases every few weeks. Or you can invest all at once and buy bonds of staggered maturities. Shorter-term bonds have smaller price swings because they're not locked in for such a long period. The principal will be returned to you as the bonds mature, and you can quickly reinvest at higher rates. And if rates are falling, you'll be less upset because part of your portfolio is still earning rates higher than those that are currently available.

It's relatively easy to buy staggered maturities of U.S. government bonds or shorter-term Treasury bills (T-bills). You can do it online at the U. S. Treasury web site, **www.treasurydirect.gov**. You can open a Treasury Direct account at the site and create instructions to automatically roll over your T-bills or bonds when they mature, getting the prevailing rates at the time. In effect, you become your own disciplined bond fund manager.

Covered Call Writing to Add Investment Income

Owning stocks for growth is an important strategy in your retirement portfolio. You can increase your retirement income by concentrating on shares of companies that pay dividends. You can also increase your investment income by writing covered call options to collect more income on stocks you already own.

Most people think options are confusing, and perhaps risky; but quite the opposite is true if you use conservative strategies that actually minimize your investment risk. As noted in Chapter 9, call and put options give the buyer a chance to control shares of stock for a specific period of time without a large outlay of cash. For a small premium, the call buyer gets the right to purchase (and the put buyer gets the right to sell) a stock at a specific strike price for a limited period of time. If the stock doesn't move beyond the strike price, the option expires worthless and the option buyer loses the cost of the option.

The person who grants that call option to the buyer is likely to be an individual with a portfolio of stocks who is searching for more income from the portfolio. If an investor writes, or grants, a call option, she collects the premium as income.

When you write a call option, there are only a few things that can happen. If the stock goes down or stays at about the same level, the option will expire worthless. You—the call writer—keep the stock *and* the premium income. The extra money you received for writing the call will cushion any stock losses. If the stock goes up, the person who bought the call will probably exercise the option and demand delivery of the stock at the promised strike price. You won't complain, though, because you sold the shares at a price you thought acceptable when you wrote the call. And now you have more money to invest in more stocks, which allows you to write more calls and to earn more premiums.

You can start a program of call writing by purchasing individual stocks. (A call option can only be written against 100 shares.) You'll probably want to diversify your call-writing program over many stocks. The easiest way to do so is to buy 100 shares of an exchange-traded fund (see Chapter 9), a fund that represents an index such as the Standard & Poor's (S&P) 500—S&P Depositary Receipts (SPDRS), know as Spiders (ticker symbol SPY); or the Dow Jones Industrial Average—the Diamonds (ticker symbol DIA). Then you can write a call against 100 shares of your fund. The premium you take in boosts your investment income. The costs of ETF transactions can cut deeply into your income. But if you execute the trades at a deep-discount brokerage that specializes in this type of activity, you can pay as little as $1 in commissions for each 100 shares of the ETF and the same small commission for each option contract written.

In fairly steady markets, studies show that this strategy could easily add as much as 6 percent or more to an index fund investor's total return. In strong markets, the return could be even greater, although the written option limits the investor's gain on the upside. In a declining market, the call writer who gathers premium income will lose less than the buy-and-hold investor will—and may even earn a small profit. But in a real bear market, you may still have big losses on the underlying stock.

For information on this strategy, visit the Learning Center at the Chicago Board Options Exchange's web site—**www.cboe.com**. Also, I highly recommend a book that's designed specifically to teach individual investors how to write covered calls: *Create Your Own Hedge Fund with ETFs and Options,* by Mark Wolfinger (Wiley, 2005).

Thus far, we've concentrated on creating your own income in retirement. But generations of Americans have relied on the promise of Social Security benefits as a foundation for their retirement income. After all, we've paid into the system over our entire working lives. As you'll see in the next chapter, many current retirees depend almost completely on that monthly check from the government to live in retirement.

In every discussion of Social Security reform, it has been promised that benefits will continue uninterrupted for current retirees. But will those promises extend to the baby boomer generation over the next 40 years? It's important to understand just what you can expect from Social Security and what some of the changes might be in future years.

INCOME RESOURCES

www.irahelp.com   Ed Slott, IRA expert and author of *Parlay Your IRA into a Family Fortune* (Viking, 2005), answers individual questions on IRA issues at his web site.

www.treasurydirect.gov   Create a portfolio of U.S. Treasury bills, notes, and bonds.

www.cboe.com/learning center   Learn about covered call writing.

www.seniorjobbank.com   For job seekers over 50.

www.aarp.org/money/careers/findingajob   Shows you how to locate a Senior Community Service Employment Program (SCSEP) in your area.

www.snagajob.com   This web site for part-time and hourly jobs has a special section for seniors.

CHAPTER 12

SOCIAL SECURITY AND MEDICARE

If you're a baby boomer, Social Security can't possibly provide for you in the same way it provided for your parents. That's a simple statement of fact. Even though we of the boomer generation have paid into Social Security at high rates throughout our working lives, there are simply too many of us. The money we paid in has been used to pay our parents' current benefits, and there aren't enough younger people to take care of us in the same style.

SOCIAL IN-SECURITY

This is no secret! Here's a quote from the Social Security Administration's web site—**www.socialsecurity.gov**:

> Unless action is taken soon to strengthen Social Security, in just 14 years we will begin paying more in benefits than we collect in taxes. Without changes, by 2041 the Social Security Trust Fund will be exhausted. By then, the number of Americans 65 or older is expected to have doubled. There won't be enough younger people working to pay all of the benefits owed to those who are retiring. At that point, there will be enough money to pay only about 73 cents for each dol-

lar of scheduled benefits. We will need to resolve these issues soon to make sure Social Security continues to provide a foundation of protection for future generations as it has done in the past.

The facts are finally being publicly acknowledged and solutions debated. But solutions require political consensus, which is difficult to achieve. Even with promises to leave benefits unchanged for those presently over age 55, there is still a risk that inflation—and the basis on which it is calculated—will make that promised monthly check worth less to future retirees.

When it comes to planning your retirement income stream, you need to be a realist. So here's the most realistic approach you can take: Don't rely on Social Security for more than a minimal contribution to your retirement income. There are currently about 33 million retirees receiving Social Security benefits. Two out of three retirees count on Social Security for at least half their income.

In the future, the need for benefits will be just as great and will last longer as boomers' life expectancy increases. In spite of increased payroll taxes on current workers, it's likely that future legislation will further delay the age at which you can collect full benefits, will reduce benefits, or will restrict Social Security payments to those of modest income and assets. And those promised retirement checks are likely to be an ever-smaller contributor to a reasonable retirement lifestyle.

How Much Can You Expect?

Every year, workers and former workers receive a statement from Social Security that details reported earnings and gives an estimate of benefits. It's important to check the reported earnings to make sure that your employers have the correct Social Security number and that you are being credited for all your wages. But unless you are planning to retire in the next few years, the statement of benefits has very little meaning.

If you haven't received a statement recently, you can use the calculator on the Social Security Administration's web site to get an estimate of your monthly benefit, based on your birth date and lat-

Table 12.1　Projected Monthly Social Security Benefits

Retirement Age	Monthly Benefit Amount*
62 years and 1 month in 2017	$1,470
66 years and 2 months in 2021	$2,007
70 years in 2025	$2,659

*Assumes no future increases in prices or earnings.

est year's earnings. (The calculator is not linked to your personal earnings history.) You'll need to have worked enough years to earn credits to get your Social Security benefit. Benefit calculations are based on an average of 35 years of earnings.

If you use the online calculator, you'll see that you have a choice of retirement years. Boomers may retire early at age 62 years and 1 month. Full retirement benefits no longer start at age 65, but at age 66, or even at 67, depending on your year of birth. Some people may decide to postpone taking benefits until age 70, at which point the benefit will be slightly larger. Once you reach age 70, there is no additional financial benefit to waiting to collect your benefits.

For example, a 50-year-old (in 2005) who had earned the maximum in Social Security covered earnings over the past 35 years might expect benefits (in 2004 dollars) like those listed in Table 12.1.

What's the best age to start taking benefits? If you start taking benefits early—at age 62—your monthly check will be about 20 percent lower than at full retirement. For those born in 1960 and later, the reduction becomes greater for early retirees, rising to a maximum of 30 percent at age 62. The calculator on the Social Security Administration's web site can tell you the breakeven point to help you determine whether to wait and collect a larger monthly benefit. A sample computation is shown in Table 12.2.

The other part of the answer depends on your longevity outlook. As Clint Eastwood asked, "Do you feel lucky?" If you think you'll live well into your eighties, it might pay to wait before you start collecting benefits. On the other hand, there's that old saying about a bird in the hand—not to mention that today's boomers might want to start collecting those promised checks while there's still money to fund them!

Table 12.2   Benefits Breakeven Points

Retirement Ages Considered	Breakeven Age
62 years and 1 month versus 66 years and 2 months	77 years and 4 months
62 years and 1 month versus 70 years	79 years and 9 months
66 years and 2 months versus 70 years	81 years and 9 months

How Much Can You Earn?

This book is based on the premise that you'll probably have to continue working if you want to maintain your standard of living in retirement. For many years, Social Security penalized those who continue to work while receiving benefits, reducing their checks by $1 for every $3 earned. This disincentive ended with the passage of the Senior Citizens' Freedom to Work Act of 2000.

Now, only those who take early benefits at age 62 are penalized by reductions in their monthly check. If you start taking benefits at age 62 but continue to work, your check will be reduced by $1 for every $2 you earn above the annual limit (which is $12,960 in 2007). Once you reach full retirement age, there is no penalty for continuing to earn money. You can now earn as much as you want without losing any Social Security benefits, starting with the month you reach full retirement age. However, if you do work at a job that is covered by Social Security after you start receiving benefits, you and your employer must still make the appropriate contributions to Social Security and Medicare out of your earnings.

Your Social Security benefits may be subject to income tax, depending on your total income and a calculation called *modified adjusted gross income* (MAGI). For a single person, your benefits will not be taxable unless the total of your MAGI plus one-half of your Social Security benefits exceeds $25,000. If you are married and file a joint return, your MAGI plus one-half of your Social Security benefits must exceed $32,000 before you are liable for taxes. (Those limits may increase in future years because of inflation.) And don't think you can get around this issue by purchasing tax-free municipal bonds. For purposes of this calculation, income from tax-free bonds is included in determining modified adjusted gross income.

How to Apply for Benefits

Your monthly Social Security check will not start automatically. You must *apply* for Social Security benefits, and it's best to start the process at least three months before you plan to retire, whether at full retirement age or earlier, if you plan to access benefits at age 62.

Contact your local Social Security office at the beginning of the year in which you plan to retire. You can apply in person, online at **www.socialsecurity.gov** or on the toll-free phone line at 800-772-1213, Monday through Friday between 7 A.M. and 7 P.M

MEDICARE

This part of the book is about streams of income, but it's important to insert a note here about Medicare, which will probably be your primary source of medical coverage once you reach age 65. Since health care will be one of the largest expenses in your retirement budget, it's important to get started in Medicare correctly. It's equally important to understand that the problems facing Medicare will dwarf the headlines about Social Security.

The Employee Benefit Research Institute (EBRI) projects that over the next 75 years Medicare's unfunded liability will be more than seven times greater than Social Security's gap—nearly $28 trillion, as compared with $3.7 trillion for Social Security. Prescription drug benefits are expected to add another $720 billion in costs over the next decade. At the current rate of promised benefits, EBRI estimates that the Medicare trust fund will begin declining in 2010 and will be exhausted by 2020. In the meantime, it's estimated that by 2030 more than 77 million people will be eligible for Medicare.

Medicare's financial woes present a different type of challenge to retirees. While you can save more and invest more aggressively to supplement declining Social Security benefits, it's almost impossible to plan enough funding for future health-care costs. Once again, living longer and having expensive treatments to prolong life can wreak havoc on the best retirement plans.

Medicare spending is projected to surpass Social Security spending in 2024 and to take a 7 percent share of the federal budget by 2030—up from about 3 percent now. At some point, the nation will have to face up to the costs of health care and decide whether it must be rationed. In the meantime, if you're facing retirement, you must plan carefully to take advantage of the current benefits offered by Medicare.

Medicare Enrollment

Enrollment in Medicare is automatic at age 65 once you begin to receive Social Security benefits. But boomers, whose full retirement benefits from Social Security don't start until age 66 or 67, will have to be proactive to enroll. That is done through your local Social Security office. Medicare still starts at age 65, even if you are not eligible for Social Security until age 66 or 67, and even if you decide to delay taking Social Security benefits until age 70. You should start the application process at least three months before reaching age 65, even if you are still working and covered by your employer's health insurance. Applying for Medicare in the very first month you are eligible has an impact on your eligibility for the best Medicare supplement policies.

If you retire before age 65, you may have a gap period in your health insurance. Ask your employer about continuing the company coverage through COBRA. You can search for temporary health coverage at **www.ehealthinsurance.com**.

How Medicare Works

Here's a quick look at just what Medicare covers and how it is designed. For more information, go to **www.medicare.gov** or call 800-MEDICARE, 24 hours a day, seven days a week, for personal assistance in English or Spanish. The examples below are for the original Medicare coverage, which gives freedom of choice in physicians and hospitals that accept Medicare. There is also a program called Medicare+Choice, now known as Medicare Advantage, which works like a preferred provider organization (PPO) for Medicare, somewhat limiting patient choice to a network of physicians but also eliminating the financial burden of most co-payments.

Medicare has Part A and Part B. Part A helps pay for necessary medical care and services given by Medicare-certified hospitals, skilled nursing facilities, skilled care provided by home health agencies, and hospices. It does not cover doctor visits or prescription drugs. (In spite of the reference to home health agencies, this coverage does not include custodial care, which is why Part Five of this book, on long-term care insurance, is so important.)

Although there is no cost for Part A of Medicare, there is still a 20 percent co-payment required for most services. For that reason, many people choose to buy a Medicare supplement, or Medigap, policy.

Part B of Medicare helps pay for doctors, outpatient hospital care, ambulance transportation, and a variety of other tests and services, including some home health care when medically necessary. Part B pays 80 percent of most covered services. You are responsible for the other 20 percent. If you are treated by a doctor who bills for more than Medicare is willing to pay, you might have to pay the difference.

There is a monthly fee for Part B, adjusted upward each year. The monthly amount could be higher if you do not sign up for Part B when you become eligible. That amount is typically deducted from your Social Security check. However, if you are not yet receiving Social Security checks, you can arrange to be billed quarterly.

Medicare Supplement Policies

Medicare only covers services if you are sick or injured. As noted earlier, it does not cover all services in full. Most services require a co-payment, and there is a $100 annual deductible for services under Part B. There is also a limited number of hospitalization days paid under Part A. And although Medicare now covers many preventive services (mammograms, prostate cancer screening, bone density tests, etc.), it does not cover routine physical exams, dental care or dentures, cosmetic surgery, routine foot care, hearing aids, or glasses.

As generous as Medicare seems to be, it is worthwhile to purchase a supplemental policy to fill in the gaps. These are known as Medigap policies. Decades ago, the offerings from various insurers were so confusing that they were nearly impossible to compare. To simplify matters, the various supplemental policies were codified into 10 standard coverages ranging from option A to option J, each with incremental coverage and costs.

You should apply for a Medigap policy immediately after registering for Medicare Part B. (If you are 65 and still working and using your employer's health plan, you can apply for a Medigap policy when you apply for Part B during open enrollment.) During the six-month period after you enroll in Part B, you cannot be turned down for even the most generous policies because of previous medical conditions. If you don't buy this supplemental policy during your six-month open enrollment period, you may not be able to get the coverage you want later, or you may have to pay a higher price. Always make sure to pay the premiums on time, because you'll never get coverage this good at this price in the future!

If you are enrolled in Medicare+Choice, you won't need a supplemental policy because all charges are covered in this plan. If you think you might switch back to traditional Medicare, you'll want to maintain your Medigap coverage, even though there are special provisions for those who switch back.

Medicare Prescription Coverage—Part D

When you become eligible for Medicare at age 65, you must sign up separately for Medicare Part D—the prescription drug program, which is actually offered by private insurance companies. Even if you are not taking prescription drugs when you reach age 65, you should sign up for an inexpensive plan. Otherwise, you will pay a penalty on monthly premiums in future years, when you may need Part D coverage.

You do not have to get Part D coverage if you have comparable "creditable" retiree health coverage from your company or union. If that coverage subsequently ends, you can sign up for Part D later without penalty. If you have prescription coverage through the Veteran's Administration, you do not have to sign up for Part D. But the VA does not cover all prescriptions, so you might need both.

Don't get caught up in the complicated terms of the Part D plan, such as deductibles and "donut holes." The simple—and only—way to find out which plan is least expensive and most manageable for you, is to go to www.Medicare.gov and click on the "Plan Finder" tool. You'll need a list of your prescriptions, including exact dosages, your Medicare number, and your Zip code. Then with a click of your mouse, you'll find the least expensive overall plan. Federal and state assistance is available for low-income seniors.

A Final Thought about Social Security and Medicare

It's a basic Savage Truth: The government has promised more benefits to more people than it can possibly provide, even by raising taxes. When making retirement plans, you must take these government promises with the proverbial grain of salt—or even a handful.

Social Security alone will not provide an adequate standard of living in retirement. You simply must save more. When it comes to health care, Medicare will remain the most important source of coverage. But the most important thing Medicare does *not* cover is long-term custodial care, and that is a cost that could devastate even the most-well-funded retirement plan. So I've devoted Part Five of this book to the importance of understanding—and insuring against—the costs of long-term care.

GOVERNMENT BENEFIT RESOURCES

www.socialsecurity.gov   800-772-1213

www.medicare.gov Complete and easy explanations of the Medicare program, eligibility, coverage, and answers to all questions.

www.medicarerights.org Independent advocacy and policy group offers up-to-the-minute information and answers to your questions in English and Spanish.

CHAPTER

13

ANNUITIES FOR INCOME AND TAX- DEFERRED GROWTH

One of the most important aspects of retirement income planning is the need for certainty. That's part of the appeal of the Monte Carlo process, a computerized evaluation of the likelihood that you will reach your goal of not running out of money before you run out of time (see Chapter 4). But you also need the certainty of having enough regular income to cover your retirement lifestyle. That's where annuities can play a role.

When you're planning your retirement, the topic of annuities is bound to come up. Annuities do have a place in most retirement plans. Immediate annuities can provide a regular, fixed stream of monthly income. And while you're still working, tax-deferred annuities can be a place to build tax-deferred growth when other options such as 401(k) or 403(b) plans or individual retirement accounts (IRAs) have been maxed out.

IMMEDIATE ANNUITIES

An *immediate annuity* promises a check every month either for life (or for two lives) or for a fixed number of years. The amount of the monthly annuity check is based on your age and life expectancy, current interest rates, and the rate the insurance company expects to earn on the money.

When you die, the checks stop and the insurance company keeps the balance in the account. You can arrange for the checks to continue beyond your lifetime to cover the life of your spouse or heir or to last for at least a certain period of time. You'll get less money in your monthly check if you make the insurance company promise to pay not only over your life but also over a second life, or for a definite period of time to your heirs, even if you die early.

Most Monte Carlo modeling scenarios will recommend that at least a portion of your retirement fund be devoted to this secure stream of income, especially if you don't have a regular monthly pension check or if your Social Security check does not provide enough protection for basic living expenses.

The downside of an immediate annuity is that once you *annuitize* —once you start taking monthly checks—you can never access your principal again or change the amount of the check. If inflation comes along and your monthly check doesn't cover future expenses, you're stuck with that same monthly check. Of course, you want to make sure you buy your annuity from a sound, highly rated insurance company because only state guarantee funds back these promises, not federal deposit insurance.

Once you have decided how much cash to invest in an immediate annuity, it pays to compare the monthly annuity amounts offered by different companies because they may use different assumptions. To use an easy online calculator to find out the amount you could receive monthly in an immediate annuity for your life, for joint lives, or for a guaranteed certain period, go to **www.immediate annuities.com**.

There is such a thing as an immediate *variable* annuity, where the money is invested in a mutual fund-like subaccount and your monthly check varies, depending on how your investments perform. But that uncertainty belies the real reason most people opt for an immediate annuity: the peace of mind that comes from knowing that a regular monthly check will arrive in your mailbox or be deposited into your checking account.

And there is an *immediate annuity with inflation protection*. The

Vanguard Lifetime Income Program (800-662-7447) solves the problem of inflation by adjusting payments over time to reflect changes in the consumer price index (CPI). You are guaranteed a minimum payment that will never decline in absolute terms or in relative terms to inflation. Every year on January 1, payments are adjusted upward. If the index were to decline, your monthly check would not be made smaller.

The cost of this protection is embedded in the monthly payment, which is initially smaller than you would otherwise get in an immediate annuity. For example, at current rates as of this writing, a 65-year-old male depositing $100,000 in a standard immediate annuity could expect a lifetime check of about $654 per month. The inflation protection program would reduce the monthly check to an initial $423 per month, although the amount would increase with inflation. If there were 20 years with an average CPI increase of 3 percent annually, the monthly check would grow to $763. It would grow to $926 if inflation averages 4 percent over a 20-year period. There's a big difference in your check when you pay for inflation protection. That should make you aware of the potential impact of inflation on a fixed monthly check.

TAX-DEFERRED ANNUITIES

Tax-deferred annuities should be used for additional retirement savings after traditional methods have been used. Your company retirement plan contributions reduce your taxes each year, and you might even get a matching contribution. But tax-deferred annuities are funded with after-tax money, although they do provide tax-deferred growth.

With a tax-deferred annuity, you give the insurance company a check now and the insurer invests it, with all the growth compounding tax deferred. Eventually, you can take the money out, either in one withdrawal or in any amount you choose at any time. Or you can take the monthly check for life.

If you take money in one or more withdrawals, you'll pay ordinary income taxes *on the gains*. The first withdrawals are always considered ordinary income, and ultimately you can withdraw your original investment tax free. If you take a check a month for life, a portion is taxed as ordinary income and a portion is taxed as return of principal.

There are two more considerations with tax-deferred annuities that might make you think twice before buying. The first is *surrender charges.* Although these charges can be as high as 20 percent, they generally start at 8 percent and decline over the years, and they may last as long as the first eight years you own the annuity. The second concern is the federal rule that says withdrawals of earnings from tax-deferred annuities before age 59½ face a 10 percent *federal tax penalty.* So tax-deferred annuities are best for people over age 60 who don't need their principal for a number of years.

Some annuities do allow withdrawals of up to 10 percent of the principal each year without surrender charges. There are other hardship considerations that make the annuity more liquid, but you'll have to read the fine print! Basically, if you're considering a tax-deferred annuity, you'll want to be sure you have no immediate need for the money you're investing.

There are two kinds of tax-deferred annuities: *fixed-rate* and *variable.*

Fixed-Rate Tax-Deferred Annuities

These products work like bank certificates of deposit (CDs) but without the federal deposit insurance. You get the insurance company's promise of either a fixed rate for a certain number of years or an initial high rate that may be adjusted in the coming years. It's easy to compare these annuities because all the fees are figured right into the yield you have been promised.

Remember to check those surrender charges, and look for an annuity in which the surrender charge doesn't last longer than the fixed-rate guarantee. For example, you may be promised a 5 percent annual yield on principal invested for five years, with surrender charges that end after five years. That way you won't be trapped in an annuity that doesn't keep up with rising interest rates.

Variable Tax-Deferred Annuities

These annuities have subaccounts that work like a series of mutual funds inside the annuity contract. You have your choice of subaccounts, and the gains on the principal you invest result from the investment choices you make.

When considering a variable annuity, make sure if offers a good choice of investment subaccounts. There may be limitations on how frequently you can switch among the subaccounts. Be sure to ask about the annual management fees charged on the individual subaccount mutual funds.

It is very important to consider the overall cost of the annuity as well as the annual surrender charges. Many annuities have huge expenses for certain promises they make. For example, "mortality charges" promise that if you die, your heirs get the entire amount you originally invested; but you'll pay for that promise. Remember also to consider the potential cost of surrender charges.

Don't be blinded by the promise of tax deferral. If the total annual-cost package adds up to more than 1.5 percent, you might be better off investing outside an annuity in a regular taxable mutual fund. At least there, your gains will be taxed at capital gains rates, whereas gains withdrawn from an annuity are always taxed as ordinary income. And in ordinary mutual funds, you won't face steep surrender charges if you decide to take your money out and switch to something more conservative.

THE LATEST ANNUITY PRODUCTS

Insurance companies have recognized that investors are looking for security but don't want to lock themselves into fixed-rate annuities, so they developed new products that combine certain guarantees against loss of principal with some of the upside potential of the stock market. Each of these products has its costs and limitations; but, depending on your willingness to pay the price and give up some of the upside, they may appeal to investors nearing retirement who are seeking tax-deferred growth.

Guaranteed Minimum Income Benefits

The guaranteed minimum income benefits annuity is designed to grow your money on a tax-deferred basis with a real guarantee against loss and with the opportunity for stock market gains. The ultimate goal is to create a predictable lifetime stream of income along with growth of principal.

With these guaranteed minimum income benefits annuities, the insurance company offers a guaranteed rate (today around 5 percent) on the principal, typically for 10 years or more from the date of the investment. At some point in the future, your original investment, plus this guaranteed rate and any potential gains, can be annuitized into that promised check a month for life.

In spite of this annual rate promise, this is really a variable annuity. You'll have your choice of mutual fund-type subaccounts that are invested in the stock market. If the market falls, the insurance company is promising that you'll at least get your principal, plus that 5 percent annual interest if you annuitize and take a check a month for life. If the market rises, of course, you'll have gains that you can withdraw at any time after the surrender period expires, paying ordinary income taxes on the gains. If your investments perform poorly, your monthly check will be based on the original investment plus the promised interest. There is another attractive feature. If your investment choices perform well, you can lock in the higher cash value each year on the anniversary of your investment.

You pay for this minimum guarantee. The first, and most obvious, cost is a 50-basis-point charge ½ of 1 percent per year). That doesn't make much of an impact when the market is booming, but in recent years every half percent has mattered a lot.

But there's another, more subtle cost to this protection. Remember, if your investment performance is poor, you can't withdraw your original investment plus the promised minimum 5 percent interest; you must annuitize—take a monthly check for life. Well, suppose you decide to annuitize at age 70. The insurance company will likely figure your age as about 63, resulting in a smaller monthly check than you'd ordinarily be entitled to. This age reduction is called a *formula*, or *purchase factor*.

There is also an *income now* annuity. It lets you take annual withdrawals of the promised 5 percent (or whatever the rate is at the time) and leave your original investment to grow inside the tax-deferred variable annuity subaccounts. Any withdrawals are taxed as ordinary income. Later, even if there is a long bear market, you can annuitize your full original investment plus the promised 5 percent annual rate, if you wait 10 years after purchase.

Principal Protection

Principal protection is another twist on the tax-deferred variable annuity—a guarantee of protection if your investment choices within the variable annuity decline because of a falling stock market. It allows you to get back the cash you invested, subject to certain conditions, even if the value of your investment account goes to zero. It is not an income benefit, but a withdrawal benefit; and there is an annual charge against your investment returns, typically less than ½ of 1 percent.

With this annuity, you can withdraw an amount equal to your original investment, no matter what the current market value of your investments inside the annuity, as long as you do not take out more than 7 percent of your original investment every year. Withdrawals can stop, start, or be changed at any time. If you withdraw more than 7 percent of your original investment, the guaranteed principal amount will be reduced.

If the value of the annuity investment increases, you can step up the basic guaranteed value to the current contract value by paying an annual percentage charge. There are other protections that guarantee your heirs either the return of the original amount invested (less withdrawals) or the highest value of the contract during the years you held it.

This type of annuity is for people who believe they can invest in the stock market for a long period of time but want the ability to withdraw if the need arises. They also want downside protection to make sure they don't lose any of their initial investment. They are willing to pay for these features through an annual charge and their willingness to withdraw a maximum of 7 percent of their investment each year (except in extraordinary circumstances), which would reduce the guarantee of total return of original investment.

Equity-Indexed Annuities

Equity-indexed annuities offer tax deferral with features that take some of the attractiveness of fixed-rate annuities, which guarantee a certain amount of interest each year, and variable annuities, which have a return that depends on your investment decisions. In my opinion, equity-indexed annuities contain the worst features of both—typically at a high cost—and should usually be avoided.

Here's how they work. The interest you earn on the money you invest in this annuity is not fixed. Instead, it is based on the performance of some stock market index, typically the Standard & Poor's 500 Stock Index. So you have a guaranteed interest rate, combined with a chance to earn a bit extra based on the return of a stock market index. Sounds good if that's all you know, but in this case the devil is in the details.

On the downside, there is typically a floor. If the index falls, you don't lose principal. But, depending on the contract, you may not be credited with any interest. Or you may be guaranteed a floor of at least 90 percent of your original investment, along with a minimum guarantee of interest you will earn—a very low amount—even if the index falls. There are a variety of combinations, which makes it difficult to compare these products.

But it's not the downside protection that makes most of these annuities a bad deal. It's the restrictions on what you can earn on the upside to pay for that protection. You get some of the benefit of the stock market's gains, but definitely not all of the upside.

There are several ways the upside can be limited. The insurance company may set a *participation rate*, giving you perhaps only 70 percent (or even as low as 50 percent) of the total return of the index. That percentage factor might change every year, it might be guaranteed for as long as you keep your money in the annuity, or it might have a certain minimum. In any case, you're losing out on the upside potential of the stock market.

Other equity-indexed annuities provide for a *rate cap*, an upper limit on what you can earn. Even in a bull-market year, your return may be capped at 6 percent. That cap offsets the protection the insurance company offers in guaranteeing a floor—the promise that you won't earn a negative rate of interest even if the market falls. In my opinion, you're always paying too much for the protection. Of course, insurance salespeople will disagree.

The bottom line is that you might be better off with two separate annuities: (1) a fixed-rate annuity that will give you guaranteed positive interest and (2) a variable annuity that lets you capture all the upside gains on your investment subaccounts. Remember, much of the stock market's historic long-term return of just over 10 percent per year is made up of some very big years of gains that offset down years. Why limit your upside potential just because you're seeking security?

If that argument hasn't convinced you to stay away from equity-indexed annuities on principle (as well as principal), you'll want to consider the additional costs that can be packed into these products. For example, there may be an administrative fee, or margin, subtracted from your return. That could be 2 percent or more, again cutting into your upside potential. And the way the value of the index is calculated could, again, limit your participation.

Living Benefits Rider

It's understandable that you want to keep your investments growing during your retirement years, but worry about the fact that you can't replace stock market losses with new contributions—or afford to wait for years until the market rebounds. Now, some major insurance companies have recognized this retiree dilemma and come up with products that allow you the investment equivalent of having your cake and eating it, too.

Living Benefits Riders are an exiting new annuity opportunity that offer investment growth along with guaranteed withdrawals for a small extra cost. Prudential Financial and John Hancock have been the leaders in offering this product, which can be part of a new variable annuity—or, in some cases, purchased for an existing annuity product.

The Prudential "living benefits" rider promises that if you are willing to take out only 5 percent a year of a "protected value" described below, you will receive that income for the rest of your life, or your spouse's life—*even if the investments in your account decline dramatically* as a result of market activities and your withdrawals.

You decide when to start taking that 5 percent annual withdrawal. And if your money has grown to be more than your original investment as a result of your investment choices, your "Protected Withdrawal Value" will be the highest of three numbers:

- 5 percent compounded rate of return on your original investment until your first withdrawal
- Highest value your contract attained at any anniversary of your original purchase during the first 10 years
- Or the current account value.

Best of all, if you ever need to dig into the principal you've accumulated you can do so (without penalty once the surrender period has passed) and still receive 5 percent annually on the protected value, less the amount you've withdrawn. The cost could be an additional 60 basis points a year, so be sure to discuss this carefully with your annuity expert.

TAX-DEFERRED ANNUITY WITHDRAWALS

After the surrender period (and the age 59½ federal tax period) have ended, you'll be faced at some point with deciding on withdrawals from your tax-deferred annuity. Your decisions can make a big difference in how you're taxed. As noted earlier, all annuity gains are taxed as ordinary income, even if the increases came from stock market gains in your mutual fund-like subaccounts. If you set up a systematic program for withdrawals, a portion will be taxable and a portion will be a tax-free return of your original investment. This doesn't reduce the ultimate taxes (unless tax rates fall during your withdrawal period), but it does spread out the payment of income taxes.

The other tax issue arises at the death of the tax-deferred annuity holder. Immediate annuities stop paying either at the death of the owner or the beneficiary or after a certain period of time that was guaranteed at purchase. But when the owner of a tax-deferred annuity dies, the balance in the account is part of the estate. Unlike most other investments, the gain inside an annuity does not get a step-up in basis at death. Instead, the beneficiary must pay income tax on the entire gain. And, depending on the size of the estate and the tax laws at the time of death, the value of this annuity could be subject to estate taxes as well.

The obvious conclusion is that money sheltered in an annuity should be withdrawn during your lifetime, if possible. You'll want to do that in your senior years, when your income level might be lower than during your working years and you'll be in a lower tax bracket. Otherwise, if you want your heirs to get the full benefit of the variable annuity growth, you should also provide them with benefits from a life insurance policy that can be used to pay the taxes that will be due.

TAX-DEFERRED ANNUITY EXCHANGES

Before you're ready to withdraw money from your annuity, you might want to look for another annuity offering a better deal or higher rates. Once the surrender period has expired, you should look around to see what else is being offered. But don't just withdraw from one annuity, deposit the check, and buy another product. That will trigger taxes on the gains. Instead, the new insurance company will help you do a 1035 exchange to transfer directly into the new product without paying taxes. The new annuity will create a new period of surrender charges.

YOUR IRA INSIDE AN ANNUITY?

Your IRA is already tax sheltered. Why would you pay extra to purchase an annuity designed to offer tax shelter with your IRA money? There is only one reason: to use the death benefit guarantee of an annuity. That guarantee means that whatever your investment choices are inside this annuity, your heirs cannot receive less than the amount you originally invested. But there's no guarantee that you won't lose money that you need to live on during your lifetime.

Certain costs and restrictions apply when you invest your IRA inside an annuity product or when you roll over your IRA into one of these products. First, the annuity must be qualified to accept the IRA. Second, there is a cost to the death benefit. And third, the annuity itself will have surrender charges for a number of years and may limit the amount of withdrawals you can make in a single year. Consider these costs and restrictions carefully.

A qualified annuity IRA investment is primarily suitable for an individual who does not contemplate using the money to support a retirement income plan, instead leaving the asset to an heir. The same distribution opportunities apply to these IRA beneficiaries as to traditional IRAs (see Chapter 18). A spouse may inherit the IRA (either the guaranteed minimum or the account value, whichever is more) and then stretch out the withdrawals for future tax-deferred growth.

Remember, the death benefit insurance of an annuity is payable only at your death, not if your account declines because your investments declined in value. So the guarantee is useless while you're alive. The industry sells lots of annuities to IRA holders who simply feel better knowing that they can't lose their retirement money. But they won't be around to see that happy ending because it will happen only after their death.

ANNUITIES: THE REAL RISK FACTOR

Annuities are products offered by insurance companies. Although they may promise a fixed rate, they are not bank certificates of deposit. There is no federal insurance guarantee fund for money invested with an insurance company. Instead, there is a network of state funds that require companies doing business in that state to ante up cash in case of the failure of an insurance company with policyholders in that state.

The amount of coverage guaranteed by a guarantee association varies by state and by type of insurance. Here are the typical maximums: $300,000 in life insurance death benefits; $100,000 in cash surrender or withdrawal value for life insurance; $100,000 in withdrawal and cash values for annuities; $100,000 in health insurance policy benefits. That's why you'll want to make sure you're dealing with a highly rated insurance company. For insurance company safety ratings, go to **www.weissratings.com**, where you'll pay $15 for each company rating.

Now that you've seen the wrinkles involved in annuity contracts, you're probably hoping someone will come along to help you decide. And there are plenty of salespeople willing to do just that. Be sure you use trained agents that represent larger companies or use certified financial planners. Or go to financial services firms such as Vanguard, Fidelity, and USAA, which are noted for their low expense ratios. Annuities do have a place in your retirement portfolio, but you need to know their place.

ANNUITY INFORMATION AND PRICING

- **www.immediateannuities.com**
- **www.annuityinsights.com**
- **www.annuityadvantage.com**

Or for low-cost variable annuities go to major no-load mutual fund companies such as Vanguard, Fidelity, and TIAA-CREF.

INSURANCE COMPANY SAFETY RATINGS

A. M. Best Company
www.ambest.com
908-439-2200

Standard & Poor's
www.standardandpoors.com/ratings
212-208-1199

Moody's Investors Service
www.moodys.com
800-811-6980

Weiss Ratings
www.weissratings.com
800-289-9222

CHAPTER 14

HOW TO TURN YOUR HOME INTO YOUR PENSION

If you're like many Americans, your house is your largest single asset, and it's been appreciating at a rate that probably outstrips your investment portfolio. In fact, your home might represent a good portion of your retirement fund. Strategies such as reverse mortgages, installment sales, and private annuity trusts can create a regular stream of income to support your lifestyle. You invested in your home over the years. Now it can pay you back.

REVERSE MORTGAGES

Americans have always had a love affair with their homes. The baby boomers watched their parents struggle to pay off their mortgages so they could have the security of living in their own home. But now, rising property taxes and utility bills are forcing many seniors to sell those homes at prices they never dreamed of. That's fine if you want to stash the cash and are willing to rent. But if you want to stay in your home as long as possible, a reverse mortgage is the answer to a prayer. It allows you to withdraw money from your home equity, tax free, with no requirement that it be repaid until you die or move out of the home. *There is no way you can be forced out of your home.*

Reverse mortgages are made by approved lenders to people age 62 or older who have paid off their mortgage completely or have only a small balance remaining. A participating lender, such as a bank or mortgage company, will process the paperwork and give you a choice of ways to receive the money:

- You can take out one lump sum.
- You can get a fixed check a month for life, as long as you live in your home.
- You can opt for a fixed check for a set number of years, perhaps just long enough to pay off your vacation condo.
- You can get a line of credit against the equity in your home, which you can draw down as needed.

The Federal Housing Administration (FHA) insures these mortgages, which means your future stream of monthly checks or line of credit funds is guaranteed to continue as long as you live in the home. These are officially called home equity conversion mortgages (HECM).

The size of your lump-sum distribution or lifetime monthly check is determined by three factors: the current appraised value of your home, your age, and the current level of interest rates. However, there are federal limits on the total size of the loan, based on where you live. In major cities, the maximum FHA lending limit is $312,896 (in 2005) worth of equity considered for a reverse mortgage loan. Larger, jumbo reverse mortgages have no upper limits on the property value that will be considered in making the loan. But jumbo reverse mortgage loans have inherently higher interest rates than FHA reverse mortgages.

For many people, it's difficult to conceive of taking money *out* of your home without having a liability to repay that debt. But reverse mortgages are not like home equity loans. A reverse mortgage is repaid only out of the proceeds from the sale of your home after your death or after you choose to move out.

It sounds too good to be true, but it is true. And federal regulations require you to be counseled by an independent adviser such as AARP so that you will understand how this product works. Just think of it as using your house to provide your pension. All the money you poured into the house is now streaming out for as long as you're able to live there.

I can anticipate some of your questions:

How much money could I get each month?

As noted earlier, that depends on your age, location, interest rates, and the value of your home. Here's an example that is based on interest rates as of this writing. (Check with your local reverse mortgage lender for a current estimate based on your situation or use the online calculator at **www.reversemortgage.org**.)

A 65-year-old homeowner with a home appraised at $250,000 could receive either a lump sum of $137,628, net of all fees, or a line of credit for that amount. Or that 65-year-old homeowner could receive a monthly check of $807 for life. A 75-year-old could receive a lump sum of $161,029 or a $1,061 monthly check for life. You can do anything you want with the money.

Is there interest on this loan?

Yes, there's an interest rate implied in the loan, but you don't actually pay interest. Instead, the interest is applied to the balance of the amount you have withdrawn. The rate is adjusted monthly or annually, based on U.S. Treasury rates. The real impact of interest rates is on the amount you are allowed to take out of your home, as this is figured into the ultimate value of your equity. As rates go up, the amount you can initially borrow from your home goes down because the lender needs to reserve more equity against future interest costs.

How do lenders get their money back?

When you do sell your home or when you die, the mortgage company is repaid all of the money it advanced to you over the years. That includes the total of all those monthly checks plus interest that floats with market rates over the years. Any remaining balance goes to your heirs. Or your heirs can choose to keep the house and take out a new mortgage to repay the reverse mortgage loan balance.

Important note: *The repayment amount can never exceed the value of your house at the time the loan is repaid.* You or your heirs can never owe more than the house is worth when you die or when you move out and sell it.

What if I run out of equity in my home? Can I be forced to move?

No matter how long you live and how much money you withdraw, you can *never* be forced out of your home.

What if I have to go into a nursing home?

If you move out of your home for longer than one year, it can be sold, unless your spouse and co-owner is still living there. But if you just go to Florida for the winter, or spend time in a hospital, or have a short stay in a nursing home, you don't have to worry about your house being sold out from under you.

Must I give up title to my home?

Never. You retain the title to your home. But title records will reflect the amount of the loan as you draw the money down through your reverse mortgage. You still own the home, and the title to the property never transfers to the bank as long as you live in the home.

How much does it cost?

First, there are up-front fees, dictated by the FHA. There is an origination fee, which is the greater of $2,000 or 2 percent of the property value, up to the lending limit in your county. You'll also pay an FHA insurance fee of 2 percent of the total property value, up to the lending limit. That portion goes to Department of Housing and Urban Development (HUD) for the FHA insurance, which makes sure the lender will be repaid if you outlive the value of your house. There are fees and closing costs, such as appraisal fees and title and recording fees.

These fees can be substantial, but they are calculated into your net monthly check or net lump-sum withdrawal. In the previous example, on that $250,000 property, you would pay about $11,000 in fees. Of that amount, $5,000 goes to HUD, $5,000 to the lender, and the balance for appraisal fees and closing costs.

The major fees are set by the FHA. But some high-volume lenders may charge less for the appraisals, title insurance, and recording fees. Be sure to ask not only about the amount of the monthly check, but also about the fees that go into establishing that check. You're required to be given an estimate of the fees before you sign up for the loan.

Since HUD requires anyone taking out a reverse mortgage to get independent counseling, typically provided by AARP over the phone (800-209-8085), you'll have plenty of chances to ask these questions and more.

With all those fees, shouldn't I just take a home equity loan?

You may not qualify for a home equity loan based on your income in retirement, and seniors may not qualify for the lowest interest rates on a home equity loan. But most important, with a home equity loan, there will be some repayment required along the way. In the earlier example, the 75-year-old homeowner could withdraw $161,029 through a reverse mortgage, with no repayment required. But if he withdrew that amount in an interest-only (6½ percent) home equity loan, he'd have to repay $1,018 per month. That doesn't solve the problem of seniors who need cash.

What if my home is worth far more than the FHA lending limits?

A jumbo reverse mortgage is useful for properties valued at $500,000 and higher because it allows seniors to draw even more money out of their homes. The process is the same, but you're required to draw down all the money at the closing of the loan. You can deposit it in a money market account and make regular withdrawals for the spending money you need. In the meantime, you retain title to your home and the benefit of its appreciation. At your death, your heirs can sell the home and keep the excess over what you have borrowed, plus accrued interest. Once again, be assured that you cannot be forced to move out of your home.

Refer to the web sites listed at the end of this chapter to learn more about reverse mortgages and to use an online calculator to estimate your monthly check.

MORE INCOME FROM YOUR HOUSE USING TRUSTS

One of the first rules of investing is to diversify your assets, but it's hard to diversify your home without selling it. There are some perfectly legal techniques that allow you to sell your home and get it out of your taxable estate while deferring taxes on the sale.

Installment Sale

The installment sale is a real estate financing technique that has long been used for commercial properties. It also has real tax benefits for individual homeowners who want to lock in the sale at current high prices yet defer paying taxes on the gain. You can structure an installment sale with any buyer, assuming you are willing to take the risk of the buyer making regular payments. The advantage of an installment sale is that you don't pay taxes on the gains until you receive the payments.

You'll want to use an attorney who specializes in this kind of agreement, and you'll want to have a substantial down payment from the buyer—at least 20 percent—in case the buyer stops making payments and you have to foreclose. Although installment sales are frequently used for commercial property, they're not the kind of deal you're likely to make with the family home—with one huge exception. Suppose the buyer is your son or daughter, who agrees to purchase the property on an installment sale basis and rent it back to you at a fair market price while you continue to live there. Your child becomes the owner, and you receive the proceeds of the installment sale, which allows you to pay a fair rent. If you want to keep ownership of your home in the family, this is a strategy worth considering.

There are some conditions: If you sell your house on the installment plan, the buyer must begin payments to you immediately. The payments must be made in regular installments, with interest at a fair market rate. Since you are the seller, the contract means that the house is now out of your taxable estate and you've locked in the sales price. But you can stretch out payment of capital gains taxes, typically over a five-year period, as the payments come in.

An installment arrangement requires a great deal of trust between seller and buyer. In case of a family fight, the new owner—your adult child—might sell the property to someone else, repay the debt to you, and let the new buyer force you out of the home. Or your child could have financial problems and find it difficult to make payments on the installment sale or to maintain the house when repairs are needed.

Private Annuity Trust

If you're ready to sell your house (or other property) and move out, you still might have concerns about paying capital gains taxes in one lump sum. A private annuity trust can help you defer those taxes while creating a lifetime stream of income. This type of annuity has nothing to do with annuities issued by insurance companies. In this case, the homeowner creates a trust, with an independent trustee, and transfers title to the trust. The trust immediately sells the property and collects the proceeds of the sale. The trustee invests the cash from the sale of the house in safe money market investments.

The trust then pays the owner of the property not a single check for the full amount, but a stream of lifetime payments called a private annuity. The contract says that payments will go to the owner for the rest of his or her life on a regular basis, as determined by IRS life expectancy tables. When the individual dies, the payments stop, leaving nothing to the estate. Any balance in the private annuity trust goes directly to the beneficiaries, free of estate and gift taxes.

The amount of the distribution must be calculated based on the life expectancy of the seller as determined by IRS actuarial tables. The monthly check will be structured to include interest on the invested amount, at a rate determined by the IRS. The seller cannot get more than that annual amount, even if the investments in the trust increase the balance. The monthly or quarterly check is fixed at the time the trust is created. (If cash is desperately needed, it might be possible to borrow from the trust or from a bank by pledging the future stream of payments.)

The tax considerations are what make a private annuity trust so interesting. You've sold the house and locked in your profit, but you don't pay taxes until you start receiving a regular check. If you don't need the income immediately, the monthly payments from the trust can be deferred for years, as long as they start by age 70½. When you do get the check, a portion will be a tax-free return of capital.

There are three distinct taxable portions of that monthly or quarterly check the seller receives: (1) a return of capital—a proportionate share of the initial cost of the house on which no taxes are owed; (2) a proportionate distribution of capital gains from the sale of the house, which is taxed at then-current capital gains tax rates; (3) a much smaller portion that could be taxed at ordinary income tax rates because it results from interest earned by the trust on the invested capital.

With a private annuity trust, you've locked in your homeownership gains and moved that huge asset out of your estate. You've created a lifetime stream of income while assuring the balance of the asset goes to your heirs at your death. And in the process, you've delayed payment of your capital gains taxes. Now the only issue that's still up in the air is the future capital gains tax rate.

REVERSE MORTGAGE RESOURCES

Not all banks and mortgage companies originate reverse mortgages. To find a lender in your area, go to **www.reverse mortgage.org**. You can use the web site's online calculator to get an idea of the monthly amount you could receive from your home, based on your age, location, and the value of your home.

For more information on jumbo reverse mortgages, contact your local lender. You can also contact the Financial Freedom Senior Funding Corporation at 949-341-9200 or at **www.financialfreedom.com**.

PART

5

LONG-TERM CARE: THE GREATEST RISK OF ALL

CHAPTER

15

LONG-TERM CARE INSURANCE: WHO NEEDS IT?

Whatʼs the greatest risk in your financial plan? Itʼs not another bear market. Itʼs the devastating cost of long-term care. Living longer may bring with it challenges that we cannot handle on our own. We might need help with routine activities of daily living, our health might become impaired because of progressive diseases, or our cognitive ability might be limited by Alzheimerʼs disease.

We baby boomers will eventually face these problems for ourselves, but right now many of us are confronting them for our parents. Do your parents and in-laws have enough money to pay for their own care for years to come, or will you be asked to supplement their long-term care needs just when your own children are in college and you are trying to save for your own retirement? I confronted this issue early, when it became my responsibility to arrange and pay for my grandmotherʼs care. Thatʼs when I recognized the importance of long-term care insurance.

THE GOVERNMENT'S ROLE IN LONG-TERM CARE

As you can see in Figure 15.1, the big bulge in todayʼs population is in the 35 to 55 age group. Right now, we are not only supporting ourselves and our children, but we are also paying taxes to support our parents, who are already receiving Social Security and Medicare benefits. In 20 years, we'll be the older, retired generation. The graph in Figure 15.1 becomes relatively top-heavy.

Will government programs be able to care for baby boomers in their old age? Not if history is any example. Remember how crowded the public schools were in the 1950s and 1960s? Remember the temporary classrooms in trailers? That's what state-provided nursing care for seniors could look like in 20 years.

By relying on government to pay for your long-term care, you give up the choice of having home health care for as long as possible. You'll be forced into a nursing home setting just when millions of other baby boomers find themselves in the same position.

If we depend on our savings to fund the possible need for long-term care, we court the risk of running out of money. If we depend on our families, we pass on an incredible burden to our children. If we're alone, as many women will be, what happens when we run out of money? And if we depend on the state, what kind of care can we

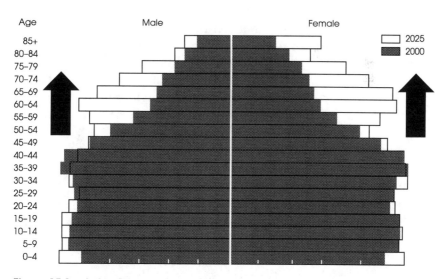

Figure 15.1   Aging Demographic: Population by Age and Sex, 2000 and 2025
Source: U.S. Census Bureau 2000, Raymond S. Kulzick, courtesy of Genworth Financial.

expect to receive? You can plan ahead, or you can take your chances. Planning ahead involves purchasing insurance to cover the cost of long-term care.

It's a common misconception that Medicare, supplemental policies, or some other government program will pay for all the costs of care as we age. Medicare pays only for a limited number of days of skilled nursing care after hospitalization. It does not pay for long-term custodial care. Medicare supplement policies do not cover this type of custodial care at all. State Medicaid plans for the impoverished do cover custodial care, but only after most assets have been used up, and primarily in facilities where you would least want to spend your last days.

Some seniors and their families mistakenly plan to become impoverished so that the state can take over their custodial care while children inherit their savings. That's a tragic mistake. Relying on state Medicaid programs limits choice and practically guarantees that you'll be forced into a state-funded facility. As state budgets get squeezed, so do reimbursements to these nursing homes. State-funded facilities are already feeling the crunch—even before the boomer generation requires assistance. What kind of care can they provide without adequate financial resources from the state?

Since Medicaid reimbursement rates are low, many private nursing homes will not accept Medicaid patients, although they will allow a resident to remain if private funds run out and a state program takes over payment. Even then, the resident may have to move from a private room to a semiprivate or onto a floor with fewer services. Stop by for a visit, and I think you'll conclude that's not where you want to see your parents—or yourself.

Your parents probably want to stay in their own home or apartment to receive care; but home health care costs money and it is not covered by Medicare, Medicare supplements, or traditional health insurance. They might want to move to an assisted living facility instead of a traditional nursing home, but those facilities can be very expensive, and the costs are not covered by the federal programs or by health insurance.

Today, 80 percent of all long-term care is provided in the home by family members. Is someone in your family prepared to take that responsibility? Could you afford qualified home health care at today's average rate of $18 per hour (or higher in large cities) to provide additional help? These are questions baby boomers should be asking for their parents and eventually for themselves.

The answer is long-term care insurance. It covers stuff we don't like to think about for our parents, much less ourselves: the need for assistance in managing the daily activities of living in our later years—bathing, dressing, or even feeding ourselves. That possibility seems so far away, and it might never happen. After all, our parents are still living vital, independent lives. That's exactly the time to make sure they have coverage. And it's the perfect time to buy coverage for yourself—while you're in your early fifties and in good health. If you can't stand the thought of ever needing this kind of care, take a different perspective. Tell yourself that you're buying long-term care insurance to give yourself peace of mind during your retirement years.

INSURANCE FOR YOUR RETIREMENT

When you own a long-term care insurance policy, you can live the retirement lifestyle you've planned without worrying about extended health-care expenses being a burden on your spouse or your family. You can expect that your retirement withdrawal scenario won't be interrupted by ongoing and expensive custodial care costs. In short, you can enjoy your retirement years without worrying about depleting your assets.

It's human nature to look in the rearview mirror in order to predict the future. That's why so many people are looking backward and worrying about another stock market decline. Ironically, that look in the rearview mirror means today's boomers are missing the oncoming disaster that is certainly facing our generation. It's the coming crisis in the cost of living longer—a cost that could devour our retirement assets. A lifetime of savings could be depleted in paying for just two or three years of nursing care.

We assess risk when we structure our investment portfolios to give us the best chance of having money to last a lifetime. It's a key ingredient in Monte Carlo modeling. And we assess risk in everyday life when we buy homeowners or auto insurance to protect the assets we've worked so hard to accumulate. Yet relatively few people are insured against the more likely risk of needing long-term custodial care. Yet the odds are you'll need that kind of help if you live long enough. More than 40 percent of Americans reaching age 65 are likely to enter a nursing home, and 10 percent of those individuals will stay five years or more, according to America's Health Insurance Plans (AHIP), the industry association.

But nursing home care shouldn't be your only option. You can have a range of choices if you have the money to pay for them. You might start with daily or twice-weekly visits from a home health-care aide. Or perhaps you want to move into an assisted living facility. Years later, you might require the 24-hour assistance that only a nursing facility can provide. So don't make the mistake of calling long-term care insurance by its old name: nursing home insurance. Your policy should cover a range of options and keep you from being forced into a nursing home except as a last resort.

Our Parents, Ourselves

It's pretty obvious that you should buy a long-term care insurance policy for yourself to make sure you have a choice of care and to preserve your assets for a surviving spouse or your children. What may not be so obvious is the need for your parents to have a long-term care policy. Although it's better to purchase at a younger age, many policies can be affordable for people in their seventies, as you'll see in the pricing examples in Chapter 17.

Bringing up the subject of long-term care insurance may reveal a huge generation gap in your family. It's possible that your parents don't know how the concept has changed in recent years—from coverage that used to force older people into a nursing home to today's policies that pay for home health care as needed. And if you are buying a policy for yourself, it might be helpful to explain to your children that you're making plans not to burden them.

If your parents won't consider, or can't afford, such a policy, adult children in the family should think about joining together to make the cost of the annual premium a gift for their birthdays, Christmas, or Mother's and Father's days. They'll think you're being generous, and you are. But it's also a hedge against your spending your own retirement dollars to care for the people who once cared for you.

LONG-TERM CARE INSURANCE: A WOMAN'S ISSUE

Long-term care insurance is a woman's issue for two reasons. First, women tend to live longer than men. In 1940, a 65-year-old woman could expect to live another 14.7 years. In 2000, that advanced to 19.5 years. And by 2040, a 65-year-old woman is expected to live another 22 years according to the actuaries. Longevity increases the odds of needing some form of long-term care.

According to a Genworth Financial report, women are the fastest-growing segment of the older population, accounting for 70 percent of the population age 85 and older. And women have a 50 percent greater chance than men of entering a nursing home after age 65, according to AHIP. Currently, 72 percent of nursing home residents are women. Claims data from Genworth reveal that increasing numbers of women have been using their policies for home health care and assisted living facilities. Those alternatives are not readily available to those who must rely on government Medicaid programs.

But there's another reason that long-term care insurance is a woman's issue: Women tend to be the caregivers for others in their life, and that takes its toll, both physically and financially. Those who leave or scale back on their jobs to take on caregiving responsibilities lose a small fortune in wages and forego retirement plan contributions and potential Social Security benefits. Having insurance coverage lifts the financial burden of caregiving and ensures that caregivers can accumulate assets to provide for their own future care.

Needing care when you're older is a nagging worry for women who don't have insurance to cover the costs. While 88 percent of men say their spouse will take care of them if they become ill or disabled, only 72 percent of women figure their spouse will be able to care for them. Futurist Ken Dychtwald projects that today's American woman will spend more years caring for aging family members than she did caring for her own children! What—and who—will be left to care for the widow or single woman? The fear of becoming a bag lady is not unfounded. That's why long-term care insurance is a must for women. The cost of that policy is the price we pay for peace of mind.

And now to overcome your final objection: What if you don't use it?

WHAT IF YOU DON'T USE IT?

What if you never need help with the daily activities of living? I fervently wish that for you, and for myself. But we never complain that the money spent on homeowners or auto insurance is "wasted" because the house didn't burn down or we weren't in an auto accident. Why complain if you never use your long-term care policy? *Once you reach age 65, the chance that you'll need long-term care is 10 times greater than the chance that your house will burn down!*

We are living longer. In 20 years, there will be more than 250,000 Americans over the age of 100, triple the current number. Replacement parts—hips and knees—will allow more years for golf and fewer years with canes, walkers, and wheelchairs. Heart surgeries and angioplasty will prolong an active life and reduce sudden cardiac deaths. Even so, at some point we're likely to need help with the basic activities of life. While living longer is the best alternative, it is not without its own costs. Buying long-term care insurance is like betting on yourself to survive.

But just as you can't wait to buy fire insurance until you smell smoke, you can't wait to purchase long-term care insurance until you need the care. Not only do these policies cost exponentially more as you grow older, but at an older age you might not qualify for the coverage you want.

LONG-TERM CARE—THE FACTS

$70,080 = Average annual cost of nursing home care in a major city (2004).

$192 = Average daily rate for a private room in a nursing home (2004).

$169 = Average daily rate for a semiprivate room (2004).

$18 = Average hourly rate for nonskilled home health aides provided by a home health-care agency.

2.4 years = Average length of stay in a nursing home.

9 million = Number of Americans who have purchased long-term care insurance.

89 percent = Percentage of Americans between the ages of 45 and 64 who are uninsured for long-term care.

77 percent = Percentage of Americans over 65 who are uninsured for long-term care.

1 of 5 = Number of households providing care to an adult family member.

60 percent = Percentage of boomers who will need some form of long-term care after age 65.

CHAPTER 16

HOW TO
UNDERSTAND
LONG-TERM
CARE
COVERAGE

By now, I hope you're convinced that a long-term care insurance policy is an important part of your financial plan. But that still leaves some questions about the policy itself: What does it cover? How much coverage do you need? When should you buy it? What should it cost? These are issues you need to understand before you make your purchase.

This sector of the insurance industry is changing so quickly that I recommend you consult an agent who specializes in long-term care insurance. Some agents represent only one insurance company. Other independent agents can show you policies and prices from several different insurers. You can even get price quotations online, although you'll have to complete a detailed application, which typically requires working with an agent.

One thing is certain: You'll want to buy a policy from a large company that has shown its determination to be a force in the long-term care industry. You might need an agent different from the one you've worked with on homeowners or auto insurance, or you might find that the best long-term care policy does come from your current insurer. Comparisons are a must, but the project doesn't have to be complicated if you work with an agent you can trust.

Let's start with some perspective on the care costs you may need to cover—now and in the future.

RISING DEMAND, SOARING COSTS

Health-care costs are rising across the board, with nursing home costs leading the way. In spite of an almost universal wish to stay *out* of traditional nursing homes, more and more people are requiring the care they provide. The financial burden can be catastrophic.

The average annual cost for nursing home care is about $70,000, according to a 2004 MetLife survey—more than $192 a day for a private room. In major cities, the cost can be 20 percent to 40 percent higher than in smaller towns, according to a Genworth Financial review. And although the average stay in a nursing home is less than three years, patients with dementia or Alzheimer's might need care for eight years or more.

Home health care can be even more expensive—an estimated $180 for a 10-hour shift. Purchased on an hourly basis, certified home health-care aides may charge more than $24 an hour in urban areas. The next step might be an assisted living facility, but that can be an equally expensive alternative and is available only to those who need limited care.

What if care is needed on a 24-hour basis? Dementia or multiple incapacities eventually wear down the most determined caregiver. A nursing home becomes the best alternative. Call a few facilities in your town and ask about their rates. Then imagine yourself searching for care for your parents or spouse. It's a tough enough decision to make, without considering price. Insurance allows you to focus on the emotional issues.

Costs for all types of custodial care have been rising at twice the rate of consumer price inflation. Month over month, those costs can add up to a staggering sum. There are about 18,000 accredited nursing homes in the United States. If supply and demand are allowed to work their economic magic, care prices will continue rising as boomers age, even if more nursing homes and other resources are added to the supply.

WHEN TO BUY? WHILE YOU CAN!

The need for long-term care immediately conjures up pictures of much older people, dependent on walkers and wheelchairs. Since that won't be you for a very long time, if ever, there's an inclination to put off buying insurance, to think about it tomorrow. That could be an expensive mistake.

Surprisingly, we may need long-term care even before we enter our retirement years. In fact, more than 40 percent of the 13 million people currently receiving some form of long-term care are between the ages of 18 and 64, as a result of accidents, stroke, or disabling disease. That's one good reason to think about long-term care insurance now, as you reach age 50, or even earlier. Today you are healthy and independent. All that could change in a minute, and it's not just a question of aging. The idols of our youth are examples of that possibility.

Even "Superman"—Christopher Reeve, whose horseback riding accident left him a quadriplegic at age 43—needed years of expensive care before his death in 2004. Disney Mousketeer Annette Funicello has been confined to a wheelchair with multiple sclerosis (MS) for years. (If Britney Spears is your Mousketeer, then you should be telling your parents to buy a long-term care policy!) Michael J. Fox functions well, for now, with Parkinson's disease. Think of the costs of long-term care for President Reagan, who suffered from Alzheimer's for more than a decade. While we hope that research will restore spinal function, cure MS and Parkinson's, and delay Alzheimer's, we must insure against those possibilities.

Because the original purchase price of a policy rises exponentially with age, the younger you are when you purchase one, the less it will cost. Insurance companies used to lock in the premium, based on your age at the time of purchase. These days, although they may project that the premiums will remain level, insurers reserve the right to increase premiums on all policies of that same category in any state. Still, it's worth buying your policy while you're young (in your early fifties) and healthy because you never know when an accident or illness will disqualify you from coverage.

Figure 16.1 shows the cost of procrastination. If you buy at age 50, your annual premium could be $2,254. The same policy coverage would cost $3,895 if you wait until age 65.

The long-term care insurance market is changing quickly as insurance companies look at the aging population and analyze the increasing costs of extended care. Companies that were pioneers in selling long-term care insurance are redesigning their policies and offering new buyers limited benefits at higher premiums. Insurers are becoming more stringent in their health and cognitive examinations, and there is a growing list of medical conditions that limit an individual's ability to obtain long-term care insurance coverage at preferred prices or, in some cases, at any price.

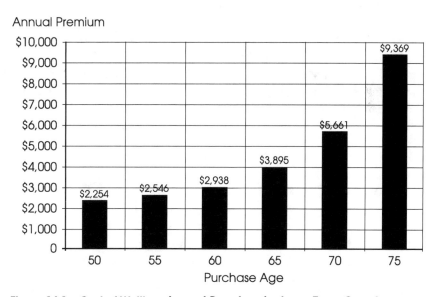

Figure 16.1 Cost of Waiting, Annual Premium for Long-Term Care Insurance
Source: Chart created by MAGA Limited based on hypothetical client information. Premiums vary based on benefits, age, health, and state of residence.

How Do I Use My Policy?

Before talking about the coverage you need, there's an important aspect of long-term care insurance policies you must understand. Unlike a life insurance policy that pays your beneficiaries when you die, a long-term care policy pays benefits you use while you're alive. But what triggers the benefits? What makes the insurance company *start* paying caregivers?

If you have a long-term care policy, the need for care must be certified by a physician. Your doctor must certify that you will need help with at least two of the six activities of daily living for at least 90 days. "Activities of daily living"(ADL) is not just a casual phrase. It refers to specific activities that are defined by insurance policies. They are *bathing, dressing, eating, toileting, continence,* and *transferring from bed to chair.* A policy can also be triggered by a physician's certification of cognitive impairment, ranging from the onset of Alzheimer's to dementia. Depending on your policy, you can access the care at home or in a nursing home or assisted living facility after a specified elimination period.

It's difficult to imagine that someday you might not be able to move from bed to chair or that you might need help in the bathroom. It's equally depressing to think that you could suffer from Alzheimer's and require extensive supervision. But what's hardest to accept is that you might have to pay someone $200 a day—or far more in 20 years—to assist you in basic daily living activities. That's why you own a long-term care insurance policy.

What Should My Long-Term Care Policy Cover?

Comprehensive long-term care insurance policies typically cover nonskilled, skilled, and custodial care in your own home or in an assisted living facility, adult day care center, or nursing home. You can lower the cost by purchasing a policy that doesn't cover home health care, but I would not recommend cutting costs in that manner.

All policies are not alike, so you will have to choose among certain features. Understanding the choices is essential to ensuring that you get the type of protection you'll need. Following are the most important options to look for in your long-term care policy.

Elimination Period

Just as you have a deductible on your car insurance, there will also be a deductible period—a waiting, or elimination, period—during which you must pay for services before the long-term care insurance policy kicks in. Typically this is a 90- or 100-day period. Choosing a longer elimination period can lower the premiums. After paying for services for those first three months, you'll be glad you purchased a policy for yourself, your spouse, or your parents.

Daily or Monthly Benefit

Choosing a specific daily benefit is the most common way to define the amount of coverage to buy. You'll want your policy to have at least $200 a day in coverage; but if that makes the policy too expensive, it's better to have a smaller amount of coverage than none at all. After all, you will still have some assets of your own to contribute to your care.

Make a few phone calls to check the costs of nursing homes and home health-care agencies in your area to make sure you are buying adequate coverage. Some companies allow you to choose an amount of monthly coverage. For example, $6,000 per month coverage would allow you to have part-time home health care a few days a week, costs that might exceed a daily benefit. Most policies offer a pool of benefits. That means that although the maximum payout would be $200 a day, if you don't use that coverage on a daily basis, the remainder stays in a pool of unused benefits that can be used to extend the coverage period.

Length of Benefit

Your policy could offer benefits for a period from three years to your entire lifetime. (As noted earlier, a three-year policy could actually cover care for a longer period if the full daily benefit is not used in the early stages of care.) Lifetime coverage is very expensive, but it buys peace of mind in case of a lingering illness.

Since the average stay in a nursing home is about three years, you might choose coverage for three-, five-, or ten-year periods. On the other hand, Alzheimer's patients and stroke victims may require assistance for a decade or more. Ask your agent to illustrate prices for a range of daily benefits and lengths of benefits. Knowing what's affordable will help in your decision making. Remember, even if you can't afford extensive protection, a small amount is better than no coverage at all.

Inflation Protection

While a $200 daily benefit may be adequate today, inflation could make that amount inadequate in the future. Inflation protection is not built into your coverage, and it does cost extra; but make sure your policy has it.

There are two types of inflation protection—simple and compound. For example, $200 daily coverage today at 5 percent compound inflation gives you $864 in daily benefits in 30 years, when you might be using the benefit. If you choose 5 percent simple inflation, your benefit will be only $490 per day in 30 years. If you're young, you'll definitely want to choose compound inflation, even though it significantly increases the premium. The annual premium for a 50-year-old with simple inflation coverage would be $1,438. With compound inflation, the premium rises to $2,119.

Consider buying a lower daily benefit with compound inflation protection. Over the long run that might be more advantageous, especially for those in their fifties.

There is one additional type of inflation protection, but it can be even more expensive. Some policies allow you to increase the amount of your coverage from time to time without medical evidence of insurability. It's called a "guaranteed purchase option." If you plan to increase benefits when you're older, the cost will definitely be higher, reflecting your age at the time.

Reimbursement Policy

There are two ways the insurance company pays out policy benefits once the need for care is triggered: (1) A *reimbursement plan* has the insurance company reimburse actual costs to the care provider. (2) An *indemnity plan* has the insurance company pay you, the insured, the daily benefit specified for your policy. Newer policies are usually based on the reimbursement plan alternative.

With the daily, weekly, or monthly benefit reimbursement plan, you submit the nursing home, home health, or assisted living facility bills to the insurance company for payment. The insurance company reimburses the policyholder for the actual expenses, up to your maximum coverage. So if your daily expenses are $150 and your policy limit is $200, only the actual expenses are paid to you. If your policy limit is $150 per day and your expenses are higher, you must make up the difference. Be sure to look for a weekly or monthly reimbursement policy that allows the unused daily benefit to accumulate and be used later within a specified period for approved services.

The other alternatives are similar. An *indemnity* policy gives you a fixed daily benefit specified in your policy, but you must submit bills from approved caregivers to receive the benefit. A *cash benefit* policy simply gives you a monthly amount, to be used for any type of care or caregiver. (The physician still must certify the need for care.) The flexibility of the cash benefit policy makes it more costly.

Guarantee Period

Not long ago, people purchased long-term care policies and assumed that the prices would stay level for their lifetime. That was the implied promise, as insurance companies urged people to lock in lower prices by buying while they were young and healthy. But the fine print in many of those policies didn't actually guarantee that prices would be fixed for the buyer's lifetime.

In fact, in early 2000, insurers started taking a second look at the potential cost of the liabilities they had booked in selling their long-term care policies. They realized that unlike the previous generation of nursing home policies, which policyholders were reluctant to use, the promised benefits of assisted living in the newer polices made usage very attractive. The increased likelihood of usage meant that policies had been underpriced, so the insurers began applying to states for permission to raise rates as the guarantee periods expired.

The resulting publicity put a dent in the sales of these policies. Who wants a policy that will cost more just when you are most likely to need it and least able to afford it?

Now that the long-term care industry has consolidated, there is less chance of substantial price increases. Still, when buying a long-term care insurance policy, ask if there is a guarantee period, and look into the company's history of rate increases. Read the section on limited-pay options in Chapter 17. Although these provisions make a policy far more expensive, they eliminate concern about future price increases.

Spousal Discounts

Some companies offer discounts ranging from 10 percent to 40 percent if both spouses purchase a policy. The definition of *spouse* can be very liberal, in some cases including domestic partners, so be sure to ask. If you're purchasing a long-term care policy with a spouse, ask about a *survivorship waiver of premium*. Some policies offer this plan, which promises that if one spouse dies after 10 years of paid premiums, the surviving spouse's policy will be considered fully paid.

Intergenerational Transfers

What happens if Mom doesn't use her long-term care policy, but her daughter or son needs it? We never know in advance who might be in an accident or suffer early onset of a disease that could trigger the need for long-term care.

John Hancock recognized that possibility in offering its Family Care policy. It allows an individual to add an adult child (or a child and his or her spouse) to the same policy at very little extra cost. Intergenerational policies typically offer a maximum of 10 years of care, which is available to either of the policyholders, up to the daily limit of the policy.

If both of the policyholders need care, the benefit is split between them. Or the younger owner, seeing that the parent is likely to consume the entire benefit, can purchase an individual policy while he or she is in good health. The intergenerational nature of this policy has some added benefits.

Consider the possibilities if the policy were purchased with a mother at age 67 and a daughter at age 45, for a $150 daily benefit, with compound inflation protection. If the mother dies 20 years later without using any benefits, the daughter inherits the full coverage. But at this point, the daily benefit could have grown to $360 a day because of the inflation coverage. The premium drops to what she would have paid at her original issue age of 45. The monthly premium she must now pay reflects her original underwriting class based on her health at the time the policy was purchased.

Care Coordinators

Make sure your long-term care policies offers the services of a professional care coordinator. These extraordinary individuals help the family identify sources of home care and nursing home care, and they are indispensable in coordinating and supervising care if the family member lives at a distance from the person needing care. The cost of this service should be included in the benefits, and you'll probably want the insurance company to contract with an independent organization to provide this service, giving you a choice of individual coordinators.

Optional Riders

Waiver of Premium Obviously, if you have enough health problems to trigger coverage, you don't want your spouse or your family to worry about continuing to pay your insurance premiums. Once you start accessing benefits, you can stop paying your annual premiums if your policy has a waiver of premium feature.

Nonforfeiture If you purchase a nonforfeiture rider and pay premiums on your policy for at least three years, you're guaranteed at least some future coverage if you stop paying premiums.

Return of Premium Some policies offer a return of premium option, which says that if you've paid for a number of years without making a claim, your premium can be returned to you or your beneficiary. If you've used some of the coverage, a portion of the premium may be returned. This coverage is costly, and your money might be better spent increasing your daily benefit or purchasing a compound inflation rider.

Contingent Nonforfeiture   If the insurance company does raise premiums and you cannot afford to continue paying, the contingent nonforfeiture rider says you will continue to have some limited benefits.

International Coverage

If you plan to retire in a foreign country, make sure your policy offers coverage for care given outside the United States. Remember, your Medicare health coverage does not typically provide for care outside the United States.

Now that you know what to look for in a long-term care policy, it's time to take action. Just think how terrible you would feel if you had all this information—but no policy—just when you or a loved one needed care. In the next chapter, you'll see how to go about buying your policy.

KEY ELEMENTS OF A LONG-TERM CARE INSURANCE POLICY

- Elimination period (deductible)
- Daily (or monthly) benefit amount
- Pool of benefits
- Length of benefit
- Inflation protection (simple or compound)
- Reimbursement policy
- Guarantee period
- Spousal discount
- Care coordinators
- Optional riders
- International coverage

CHAPTER 17

BUYING YOUR LONG-TERM CARE POLICY

Let's make this simple. You agree that you need to buy long-term care insurance to protect your financial future or that you need to let your parents and in-laws know about this type of coverage so they won't be dependent on you. You've read the previous chapter and decided on the most important issues: amount of daily benefit, years of coverage, and inflation protection.

WHAT INSURANCE COMPANY SHOULD YOU CHOOSE?

Now it's time to get price quotations and make the purchase. The most important consideration here is the strength of the insurance company that offers the policy. After all, you don't expect to use the benefits for years, and you want them to be around when you need them. In recent years, several major insurers have opted out of this fast-changing industry, while others have decided to make long-term care insurance a priority.

You want to be with a company that prices its policies with a long-term perspective. They won't necessarily be the cheapest policies, but you're less likely to face increases when your guaranteed-pricing period expires.

So what companies should you consider? In my opinion, you'll want to stick with the largest, best-known, and most committed insurers. These include MetLife, Genworth Financial (the former GE Capital), John Hancock, Lincoln Benefit Life (Allstate), Mass Mutual, New York Life, Prudential, State Farm, and Northwestern Mutual. Some companies, such as CNA and Transamerica, which have stopped actively selling *new* LTC policies, continue to stand behind existing policies or transfer the responsibility to another insurer to pay future claims.

WHAT SHOULD IT COST?

Policy premiums are based on your age, your location (which determines the cost of care in your area), and your health at the time you purchase the policy. The strongest long-term care insurance companies try to hold their premiums level for many years, but there are few guarantees.

The insurance company has the right to increase the price, but only for all holders within that class of policy. In some states, insurance companies must obtain approval from the state's department of insurance before any policy premium increases can be put into effect, and the insurance company must give appropriate notification to the affected policyholders.

Table 17.1 shows sample prices for a long-term care policy with some of the most popular options, for an individual in good health, living in a major U.S. city, and purchasing at ages 50, 60, and 70. The coverage is for $5,000 a month for four years, with a 90-day elimination period. It is a preferred rate given only to those in good health.

One of the most important and often overlooked aspects of a policy is the inflation protection offered in the benefits. After all, you don't expect to use the policy for many years. And while $5,000 a month could buy excellent care today, it might not cover one week in a nursing home in years ahead. But inflation protection, simple or compound, adds substantially to the annual premium cost.

Table 17.1   Sample Prices of Long-Term Care Insurance

Age	No Inflation	Simple Inflation	Compound Inflation
50	$918.00	$1,530.00	$2,254.20
60	$1,428.00	$2,397.00	$2,937.60
70	$3,366.00	$4,998.00	$5,661.00

$6,000/month, 90-day elimination, 4-year benefit period, preferred rate, no spousal or group discount included.
Source: Chart created by MAGA Limited based on hypothetical client information. Premiums vary based on benefits, age, health, and state of residence.

As you can see in Table 17.1, the older you are when you purchase your long-term care insurance, the more it will cost. And there's no guarantee that you'll qualify at an older age. These are the two best arguments for purchasing a policy in your early fifties. But buying early doesn't necessarily lock in the premium, so you might want to consider alternative ways of paying for your policy that minimize your exposure to rate increases.

10-PAY: CONTROLLING PRICE RISK

There's always the risk that the annual premium on your long-term care insurance policy will rise. In fact, that's what's been happening in recent years, as insurance companies reconsider the rising cost of claims. A policy premium may remain level for years and suddenly increase substantially.

One way to limit the risk of price increases in future years is to purchase a limited-pay policy—one with payments lasting only 10 or 15 years. Although premiums may rise during that limited period, at least you know your coverage will be fully paid up at the end of that time. Limited-pay policies are generally much more expensive because they restrict the company's ability to implement rate increases. Still, you can arrange to pay the premiums now, while you're working and can afford the cost. Then you won't have to worry about price increases in your later years when you are less able to afford them. Several companies offer these limited-pay policies.

LONG-TERM CARE POLICIES
AND INCOME TAXES

Almost every policy sold today is considered tax qualified. That means that the policy meets basic federal requirements, so any payout of benefits will be tax free to the recipient, up to $240 a day in 2005.

Currently, self-employed individuals can deduct long-term care insurance premiums, just as they can deduct the cost of health insurance. And long-term care insurance premiums are considered allowable expenses in health savings accounts, up to certain limits based on age.

Depending on your age, you may be able to deduct a portion of long-term care insurance premiums. (Hopefully, Congress will make the entire long-term care insurance premium deductible in the near future.) Those premiums are considered medical costs, which, depending on the age of the policyholder, can be tax deductible if they are greater than 7.5 percent of adjusted gross income. In 2005, if you are between ages 61 and 70, $2,720 of your long-term care insurance premium counts as a medical expense in determining the 7.5 percent of adjusted gross income that creates a tax deduction. Over age 71, $3,400 of premium is considered a medical expense.

This web of tax provisions allows for some creative ways to reduce the after-tax cost of long-term care insurance premiums. For example, instead of paying for your parents' long-term care insurance policy, you might want to gift them an amount equal to the annual premium. If *they* pay the premium, a portion may be tax deductible for them.

The best tax deals are reserved for companies that purchase long-term care insurance for their employees. When a corporation pays for long-term care insurance for employees (with benefits up to $240 per day), the premium cost is fully deductible to the corporation and the premium paid is not considered to be income to the employee. When the employee actually uses the policy and starts receiving benefits, those payments are not considered taxable.

Partnerships, limited liability corporations (LLC), and Subchapter S corporations can fully deduct the premiums for long-term care insurance for nonowner employees. Partners or owners, however, have to take the amount of the premium as income, subject to some exclusions based on age. This interesting tax provision, while it lasts, is an opportunity to provide benefits to owners of small businesses. Unlike most other employee benefits, there is no requirement that this benefit be available to all employees.

PAYING FOR LONG-TERM CARE WITH LIFE INSURANCE

The insurance companies have come up with answers for those who worry that they won't ever use the long-term care insurance before they die. The solutions are accelerated death benefit riders and blended policies.

Acceleration Riders

As a part of or an addition to life insurance policies, these acceleration options pay benefits if the insured needs long-term care due to chronic illness or other circumstances that qualify for long-term care.

The concept allows a percentage (which varies by company and product) of the death benefit from the life insurance policy to be paid out to the policy owner for long-term care needs. Payout periods range from 24 to 48 months, based on the average time that the long-term care benefits are expected to be needed. In some policies, a terminal illness can trigger a lump-sum acceleration of benefit.

Accelerated death benefit riders provide significant flexibility in the use of the life insurance policy's ultimate benefit, but there are limitations as well. First, the monthly benefit for long-term care expenses may be less than what you would find in a separate long-term care policy, and the rider might not include home health-care options. In addition, loan interest rates could be applied once part of the death benefit is converted to paying long-term care costs. You have to carefully evaluate the limitations of the riders in order to determine if this life insurance option is right for you and your potential need for long-term care.

Blended Policies

Blended policies offer a combination of life insurance and long-term care insurance. If you don't ever access the long-term care, the assets in the policy that were reserved for this coverage can be used instead to increase the death benefit. The policy also allows you to take a portion of the death benefit to fund additional long-term care coverage. Check the policy details carefully to understand the trade-offs. These policies typically offer a wider range of long-term care options, including home health care, than the accelerated benefit riders.

Golden Rule Insurance Company, for example, offers a policy called Asset-Care, which will pay a monthly portion—your choice of 2, 3, or 4 percent—of the death benefit for care. The coverage is similar to other long-term care policies: home care, assisted living, nursing homes, adult day care, hospice care, and respite care. Any part of the insurance that is not used for long-term care expenses is preserved and distributed to the beneficiaries free of income taxes. John Hancock, Lincoln National, and New York Life offer similar combination policies.

Some life policies and blended policies offer a return of premium option, which gives policyholders a chance to recapture the premiums paid on the policy or to pass those premiums on to their beneficiaries if the benefit is not used.

Blended policies, accelerated death benefits, and other options increase the price of the underlying policy. Be sure you understand their advantages and limitations so you can determine if they are worth the price.

EMPLOYEE GROUP LONG-TERM CARE POLICIES

If your employer doesn't offer a group long-term care policy, the company is missing a terrific opportunity to include a benefit that is valuable to employees and doesn't have to cost the company a penny.

A group policy allows individuals to purchase LTC insurance for themselves or for a related family member at a discounted price and with a limited medical evaluation. The insurance can be portable; so if the employee leaves the company, the policy can be continued through individual payments. And the company can choose to make the payments for certain executives as part of a benefits plan, while other employees deduct the premiums from their paycheck.

If your company needs convincing, just ask the boss or owner to consider the cost of losing a valuable employee such as his or her administrative assistant if that person has to quit or work part time to care for an aging parent. According to one MetLife study, more than 17 percent of upper-level managerial workers who were employed while caregiving had to quit their jobs or take early retirement because of their caregiving responsibilities. A Conference Board survey indicates that the cost of replacing them amounts to about 75 percent of the annual salary costs for employees who quit.

The MetLife Mature Market study estimates that U.S. companies incur $11.4 billion to $29 billion in lost productivity annually because workers are distracted by caregiving duties. That includes costs related to workday interruptions, partial absenteeism, and elder care crises. That's why the number of employers offering some form of long-term care coverage is growing rapidly.

You've probably had a coworker in this situation. AARP estimates that nearly one-quarter of U.S. households—22.4 million—contain a family caregiver for someone 50 or older. Nearly two-thirds of family caregivers work full or part time, and more than half of them have had to make some kind of workplace accommodation. The MetLife study shows that nearly half those workers reported coming in late or leaving early. Many others took leaves of absence or turned down promotions. Clearly, from both the employer's and the employee's point of view, providing long-term care insurance as an optional benefit is simply good business.

It should be noted that premiums for group policies factor in expected average costs. If you're young and healthy and have a spouse or domestic partner, you might find lower premiums and more choices of benefits in an individual policy. It makes sense to compare; but if your employer is offering a group plan, be sure to act within the initial enrollment period, which might have more flexible underwriting standards.

THE FEDERAL LONG-TERM CARE INSURANCE PROGRAM

The country's largest employer, the federal government, is setting a good example by offering its own voluntary, long-term care insurance program to employees at a reduced group premium. The federal program, launched in 2002, was widely hailed as an acknowledgment that individuals need to prepare for the possibility that they will require custodial care. The government cannot provide that care for its own employees, much less the average U.S. citizen.

The Federal Long-Term Care Insurance Program (FLTCIP) is underwritten by MetLife and John Hancock. It is open to current and retired employees of the federal government, the postal service, the military, and their families. For information, go to **www.opm.gov** to reach the web site of the federal Office of Personnel Management. Then click on Benefits. Or, go to **www.ltcfeds.com**.

LONG-TERM CARE INSURANCE FROM AFFINITY PROGRAMS

AARP (formerly the American Association of Retired Persons) is one of the largest affinity programs offering long-term care policies at group rates to members and their families. The AARP policy, underwritten by MetLife, is available to all AARP members and their families who qualify.

The AARP long-term care insurance program has several plans. One, called My Choice, is based on an interesting concept. Instead of a daily benefit amount or coverage for a fixed number of years, this policy offers a total pool of assets or cash benefit, as opposed to a reimbursement plan. Coverage can be purchased up to $600,000, with a maximum payout of $6,000 per month. When the need for coverage arises and is certified by a physician, the money can be spent for any purpose, not necessarily medical costs. This approach trusts the individual not to waste the benefits on unnecessary expenses.

The ARRP plan offers a variety of optional benefits, depending on your state of residence, and its offerings continue to change. For information, go to **www.aarp.org** or to **www.metlife.com/aarp**.

A FINAL ARGUMENT: THE COST OF NOT HAVING LONG-TERM CARE INSURANCE

Long-term care insurance is expensive, but *not* having it can be much more expensive. Figure 17.1 shows the number of days a policy would have to pay benefits for a nursing home stay in order to equal the premiums paid on a traditional long-term care policy, assuming no premium increases in the interim. If you buy a policy as a 50-year-old, it would take you only about 10 weeks in a nursing home to recover 10 years of premiums paid. Obviously, if you wait until your sixties, the higher premiums will take longer to recoup; but it still looks like a good deal if you need the services of a nursing home. At age 60, it would take three months in a facility to recoup 10 years of premiums paid.

Now that you know the facts about long-term care insurance, it's time to make the purchase. If you procrastinate, you're tempting fate and increasing your costs. That's a Savage Truth.

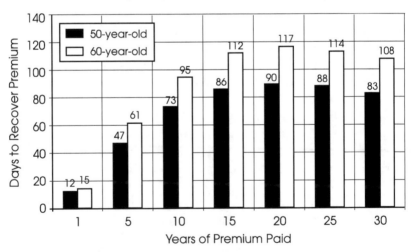

Figure 17.1   Premium Recovery, Traditional Pay   (Number of days policy will have to pay benefits to equal premium paid.)
Source: Chart created by MAGA Limited based on hypothetical client information. Premiums vary based on benefits, age, health, and state of residence.

THE SIMPLEST LTC POLICY

In late 2006, John Hancock came out with a new form of long term care policy that takes much of the guesswork out of all those choices and riders. It's called the "Leading Edge" policy and it offers coverage for 5 years, plus $1 million in extra money if you use up the pool of money from your 5 year benefit period. It that runs out, you automatically get an extra $1 million in benefits.

The result is a policy that is significantly less expensive compared to buying coverage for your entire lifetime. This policy also has built-in, compound inflation protection linked to the Consumer Price Index. When the CPI (urban index) increases, so do the benefits—on a compound basis. If the CPI decreases (which happened most recently in 1955) the benefit remains level, until the CPI rises again. For more information and pricing, contact one of the independent agencies listed below.

RESOURCES FOR PURCHASING LONG-TERM CARE INSURANCE

www.MatureMarketInstitute.com (MetLife)
www.FinancialLearning.com (Genworth)
www.gltc.JHancock.com (John Hancock)

To get price quotations and product comparisons and to find independent agents:

www.magaltc.com
www.compareltc.com
www.ltcconsultants.com
www.ltc-cltc.com

To make sure that a senior is not being pressured into unwisely transferring assets to qualify for Medicaid, find an elder law specialist in your area through:

www.elderlawanswers.com

PART 6

ESTATE PLANNING: THE PRICE OF SUCCESS

CHAPTER 18

WHAT'S LEFT?

ongratulations! It looks like your money will outlive you and you'll have some to pass on to family and friends. That's the result of smart planning. And it's the reason for this last chapter—to make sure those extra assets wind up in the hands of your loved ones, instead of in the government's pocket. If you have used up all your money in your lifetime, you still might want to leave something for your heirs, so this chapter also deals with life insurance.

Estate tax law is uncertain and confusing. Estate tax reductions are scheduled to take effect yearly, but the planned repeal of the estate tax in 2010 might not occur. In 2011, under current legislation, we could be back to the laws of a decade ago. The solution is to base your estate plan on existing law, make it as flexible as possible, and review it with your estate planning attorney at least every two years, or when you see headlines about tax changes.

As of right now, it would be best to die in 2009—if you're really planning ahead—because that is the year in which the estate tax rates will be the lowest and the dollar amount of exemptions from the tax will be the highest. If you die in 2010, the old estate tax will be replaced by a complicated system that will tax gains on assets such as stocks and your home, which previously would have been valued as of the date of your death. For those who didn't keep good records, this new system could be more challenging than the old estate tax.

Since you can't predict the date of your death, you need to structure your finances in a way that ensures your wishes will be carried out and that a minimum of taxes will be paid, no matter when you die. Just because you don't have—or don't expect to have—a lot of assets, don't make the mistake of thinking that you don't need to plan.

WHAT COULD HAPPEN?

In my speeches, I talk about a young couple who had no children and had all their assets titled in joint name. They were in a terrible auto accident. She died at the scene, and he died in a hospital a few weeks later. Since everything was titled jointly, at the woman's death her husband became the heir. When he died, everything went to her mother-in-law. (I'll let you think about that for a moment!)

If there are minor children, the situation becomes even more complicated. Without written direction, the court will be left to make the decision about who should care for them. Think you've solved the problem by leaving life insurance to them? Think again. Minors cannot be beneficiaries of insurance policies. The court will assign a financial guardian, who might take a dim view of summer camp or a car at age 16.

If you're single, depending on state laws, your parents will become your heirs. If they die soon after, your assets will be added to theirs, and much of the money you saved will go in taxes on their estate. Your brothers, sisters, nieces, nephews, and friends could have received that money if you had taken the initiative to leave written directions.

If you're living with someone but are not married, the complications can be a nightmare. You may have told everyone that your friend or partner should receive all your personal effects, but the law says otherwise. If you care, you should plan. Make it official, and make it legal.

WHAT IS YOUR ESTATE?

Your *estate is everything you own*. It's your share of your family home, if it's owned in joint name. It's your retirement plan at work. It's your car, your sports equipment, your clothing, and your jewelry. It's also your life insurance, if you are listed as the owner, even though someone else is the beneficiary.

When you add it all up, your estate might be larger than you think. Whether you've left your assets in joint tenancy or made someone the beneficiary of your IRA or 401(k), it's still your estate, and you have to deal with it while you're alive and well.

This is not a do-it-yourself project. Even the most basic estate planning requires professional help from someone who knows the laws of your state. Even so, there are a few estate planning issues you will have to address on your own before you meet with your attorney. You will want to think carefully about the important choices you'll have to make—how your assets will be distributed and whom you will entrust with that responsibility.

It's tempting to close the book right here, without taking action. But if you don't take steps to organize your estate properly, it will be laid out in full view in probate court, subject to delays and expenses, before it gets to your intended heirs. In fact, before it is given to the people you care about, it could even be subject to estate taxes.

WHAT ARE ESTATE TAXES?

You might think that estate taxes are something rich people pay at death; but when you add up your house, retirement fund, and other assets, you might very well fall into that category. The taxes kick in after the *exemption level*, which includes the value of your estate at death, plus all the gifts you've made above the allowable $11,000 per person per year. (See Table 18.1.) The rates may be as high as 45 percent on the amount above those exemptions.

Table 18.1   Exemptions and Maximum Tax Rates

Year	Estate Tax Exemption	Highest Rate
2005	$1.5 million	47%
2006	2.0 million	46%
2007	2.0 million	45%
2008	2.0 million	45%
2009	3.5 million	45%
2010	N/A (taxes eliminated)	0%
2011	1.0 million	55%

WHAT IS PROBATE?

Probate is the very public process by which the court changes title to your assets. Attorneys charge substantial fees for handling the probate of your estate. You can avoid probate by creating a revocable living trust and titling your assets in the trust. Then no judicial proceeding is required to distribute them. Some assets pass directly to your heirs anyway without going through probate or distribution from your revocable living trust. Those assets, such as retirement plans and life insurance policies, have specifically named beneficiaries. As you'll see in this chapter, choosing the appropriate beneficiary is very important.

WHAT IS A REVOCABLE LIVING TRUST?

A *revocable living trust* is a trust that you create while you are alive. You are the trustee, or you and your spouse can be co-trustees. You retitle all of your major assets—your house, investment accounts, and other properties—in the name of the trust. There is no tax consequence for this action. Your title or mortgage simply reflects that the Smith Family Trust, with John and Mary Smith as co-trustees, owns the house, instead of John and Mary Smith as Joint Tenants. You can buy or sell real property, mutual funds, or stocks in the name of the trust very easily. Any taxes on capital gains or interest are reported on your own tax return.

The revocable living trust is really useful if you become incapacitated or die. Then the successor trustee you named takes over and deals with your assets as you instructed. No court approval is required. So if you want your engagement ring to go to your daughter at your death, just put that in your trust instructions along with other assets to be distributed.

Some things you own, such as your car or your everyday checking account, you wouldn't bother to retitle. For these items, you'll need a *pour-over will*, which simply states that all untitled assets will pour over into your revocable living trust, to be distributed according to the instructions in the trust. Just remember to retitle the large, important assets into the trust name, or else they'll have to go through probate.

But you're not finished yet. There are two more key documents you should discuss with your estate planner.

HEALTH-CARE POWER OF ATTORNEY AND LIVING WILL

A *health-care power of attorney* names someone to act in matters of health-care treatment in case you are unable to make decisions for yourself. This person will authorize hospital treatment and tests and will sign waivers for surgery. A copy of this document should be in your physician's files so there is no debate about who has power in these matters.

A *living will* is what I call the "pull the plug" document. It states your wishes that treatment not be prolonged in the event that there is no chance of recovery. It's something to talk about with your family. The decision may haunt the person who has to make this call, so give careful consideration to your choice. Give your physician a copy of your living will to put in your medical file. If you've signed an organ donor card, this should also be made known to your family, and a copy should be given to your physician.

RETIREMENT PLAN BENEFICIARIES

You can name beneficiaries of your retirement plans just by signing a form with the custodian of your plan. There's no cost if you do it correctly, but it could be very costly if you make a mistake.

Your 401(k) Plan Beneficiary

Back in the days when retirees received a monthly pension check, the decisions were simple. You elected either a lifetime pension or a pension that included the life of your spouse. (Today's pension plans are required to include a spousal distribution unless the non-working spouse signs away his or her rights.) But your pension plan has probably been replaced by a 401(k) plan, and that can create problems.

You'll be asked to name a beneficiary for your 401(k) account. Get legal advice from your estate planner before doing so. Most company 401(k) or nonprofit 403(b) defined contribution plans require an immediate distribution of assets at the death of the plan participant. Since all distributions from these plans are taxed as ordinary income, an immediate distribution can trigger a huge tax bill for the beneficiary.

2006 Pension Protection Act Creates Opportunity

The Pension Protection Act of 2006 provides that, starting in 2007, a non-spouse beneficiary, such as a child or grandchild, who inherits a 401(k) plan balance can transfer that balance directly to an *Inherited IRA* that can be stretched over the beneficiary's lifetime. This transfer must be done as a direct rollover—from trustee to trustee.

The beneficiary must never actually receive a check, or the entire amount will be taxed immediately. Also the beneficiary cannot have the funds rolled into an existing IRA. It must be a newly established "inherited IRA" account, titled in the name of the deceased plan participant. Thus, the account would be titled: "Dad IRA (Deceased, January 15, 2007) FBO, son". A properly created trust may also be named as a beneficiary of a 401(k) plan.

Your IRA Beneficiary

If you die without naming a beneficiary for your IRA, you may limit the opportunity to extend the life of your IRA and keep the money growing tax free for your heirs. The rules state that if the IRA owner dies before the required beginning withdrawal date at age 70½, the money must be paid out by the end of the fifth year following the year of the IRA owner's death (the five-year rule). If the IRA owner dies *after* the required beginning date, then distributions will be calculated over the remaining life expectancy of thc IRA owner, had he or she lived. That's why it's so important to check your various retirement plans to make sure you've named a beneficiary—and that it is the most appropriate beneficiary.

Spousal Beneficiaries   If the IRA beneficiary is a spouse, he or she has two options that are not available to other beneficiaries: (1) Roll over the assets into an IRA in his or her own name, or (2) leave the assets in the deceased spouse's account. These options can stretch out the tax-deferred growth of the account.

Rolling over the assets allows them to continue to grow. If the surviving spouse is younger, distributions need not begin until he or she reaches age 70½. And that survivor's beneficiaries could later extend the period of growth of any remaining assets over their own life expectancies. A spousal beneficiary may roll over inherited assets into his or her own IRA at any time following the death, as long as the deceased spouse's required minimum distribution obligations have been met.

A surviving spouse might elect to leave the assets in the deceased owner's account if the surviving spouse is under age 59½ and wants to take distributions immediately but avoid the 10 percent federal early withdrawal penalty. Distributions from his or her own IRA would be subject to the penalty, but distributions from a deceased spouse's IRA would not be penalized.

Trusts as Beneficiaries   It's generally unwise to name a trust as beneficiary of your retirement plan because it complicates the distribution process. However, the trust's beneficiaries can be treated as if they were named individually and not through the trust if the trust meets several requirements. To meet these requirements, all of the beneficiaries must be individuals. If there are several beneficiaries, they must use the age of the oldest so that postdeath distributions on the inherited IRA can be stretched over the life of the oldest. If you're going to name a trust as beneficiary, inform your estate planning attorney of that fact and make sure the trust meets the distribution rules.

Minor Child as Beneficiary   You may want to name a minor as beneficiary in order to stretch out the future growth of your IRA assets as long as possible. But be sure your estate plan has named a guardian for that child while the child is a minor. The guardian will start taking required distributions for the minor in the year following your death, and those required distributions will be calculated based on the age of the minor. At the age of majority, the assets belong to the child—unless you have set up a restrictive trust to handle future distributions.

Nonaccepting Beneficiary   Some beneficiaries might choose to disclaim, or refuse to accept, the proceeds from a retirement account. That must be done within nine months of the death of the account owner. If a beneficiary disclaims, he or she is not permitted to name a replacement beneficiary. This decision becomes very complicated and generally requires the advice of an attorney.

WHAT ELSE SHOULD YOU CONSIDER?

There are a few more issues to think about before you meet with your estate planning attorney.

Guardianship of Children

If you're married and have young children, this is the time to sit down with your spouse and consider the possibility that both of you could die in an accident together. Who would raise your children? It's not just a question of choosing one family over the other. You need to ask now, to make sure your brother, or your husband's sister, or either set of parents would take responsibility for your children, whether or not you left enough life insurance to cover the cost.

Bequests to Minor Children

As noted, you can't just leave an inheritance or life insurance benefits outright to a minor child. You will have to set up some sort of trust arrangement to make sure the child receives the benefits, and you will have to decide at what age the principal of the trust is to be given to your child. It could be at age 18, if that's legal in your state, or age 21, or even older. You'll wield control from the grave as long as the assets remain in trust, but does that create a more responsible young adult? These are discussions to have with your spouse—and with guidance from your attorney.

Trusts for Disabled Adult Children

If you have a child with special needs, it is particularly important to get competent advice on structuring a trust that will allow the money to be used for the child's benefit as he or she becomes an adult, but does not disqualify the individual from helpful state and federal programs. It's not a question of gaming the system. Even if you have plenty of money, there are some programs you simply cannot buy into; they are restricted by law to disabled people who qualify for Medicaid. Group homes, which are a good solution for handicapped adults, often fall into this category.

Two types of trusts are appropriate in planning for disabled adult children:

- The *special needs trust* is sometimes called a 15.1 trust after that section of the Trust and Trustees Act. Money in this type of trust can be used over and above government funding, but not for basic support. Uses could include special clothes, entertainment such as movies or bowling, or other personal needs. A special needs trust must be funded with third-party money.

That means it cannot be money that is the property of the child.

- A *payback special needs trust* is also known as a (d)(4)(A) trust. It can be set up only by parents, grandparents, guardians, or the court. It is for money in the name of the person with the disability, from sources such as earnings, gifts, inheritances, or accident settlements. It can be used to support additional needs above government benefits; but when the disabled person dies, Medicaid is reimbursed out of the balance.

Division of a Business

Many books have been written on this topic because it can be so contentious. One child may have worked in your business; but if it is a major part of the estate, and you don't want your children to be forced into a sale, you'll need to consider replacing the value of the business by purchasing an appropriate amount of life insurance. That's where you'll need real expertise. The situation requires even more advance planning if you have a business partner.

MOVING ASSETS OUT OF YOUR ESTATE

If you've really been successful at accumulating assets and living within your means, you might have enough money leftover to worry about getting money out of your estate before it is subject to estate taxes. Even though the exempt limits are rising every year and there is a possibility of eliminating the death tax permanently, you'll want to develop an estate plan that can be revised later if necessary. After all, no one informs you of your end date in advance.

Estate planning attorneys specialize in coming up with ways to keep your estate from being taxed. That's why you need professional advice. But here are two simple strategies that you can employ on your own.

529 College Savings Plans to Avoid Estate Taxes

These popular plans offered by every state allow money to grow tax free for college expenses. Many families use them to save as much as they can to meet future college expenses. But 529 plans also have great estate planning applications. As noted earlier, each spouse can give $11,000 per year to any number of people without impacting the combined estate and gift tax. But the 529 plan law allows each parent or grandparent to aggregate five years of that $11,000 annual gift—$55,000 in total—and place the money in a 529 college savings plan for each child or grandchild. If one child or grandchild doesn't use the money, another child can use it for college expenses.

Very wealthy families can get a lot of cash out of their estates without creating an expensive legal trust by using a 529 plan. (Go to **www.savingforcollege.com** for information on 529 plans and your state plan.) Of course, when grandparents consider transferring large amounts of money before their death, they may worry about needing the cash in the future. If the need arises, they can withdraw the money by paying a 10 percent penalty and ordinary income taxes on any gains, much as early withdrawals on a retirement plan are treated. It's a stiff price to pay, but the money is not completely out of reach; it is, however, out of the estate.

Reverse Mortgage to Fund Life Insurance outside the Estate

Many people have a lot of their wealth tied up in the family home— a home they don't want to sell. As explained fully in Chapter 14, they can use a reverse mortgage to withdraw equity from the home that reduces the value of their estate as they spend the money, and they can gift some of the cash to their children each year.

They can also use some of the proceeds from the reverse mortgage to fund an irrevocable insurance trust that pays for insurance on their lives. When they die, the trust keeps the life insurance proceeds out of their estate. Their children receive the life insurance proceeds tax free. The heirs can pay off the reverse mortgage and keep the house. Or they can keep the life insurance cash and whatever equity is left after the house is sold and the reverse mortgage is repaid. Either way, the couple will have used the equity in their home to maximize the transfer of assets to their heirs, free from estate taxes.

LIFE INSURANCE AND YOUR ESTATE

Life insurance is a complicated subject, and I'll assume that you met with your insurance agent or financial planner long ago to determine the appropriate amount and type of life insurance. As you get older you may have more—or less—need for life insurance. It's best to plan in advance, while you are younger and insurance costs less, and while you are healthy enough to qualify.

Your original reasons for owning life insurance may disappear as your children mature and your fortune grows. But a growing retirement fortune creates its own new need for life insurance—to liquefy your estate so a family home or closely held business does not need to be sold to pay estate taxes.

What Kind of Life Insurance Do You Need?

Young families are usually best off buying inexpensive term life insurance, which can guarantee a low, level premium for at least 20 years or as long as 30 years. To get price quotations, go online to services like **www.accuquote.com**. Calculators at the web site will help you determine how much coverage you need. Term life insurance is a commodity business, with fairly standard attributes that allow easy online price comparisons. Simply choose term life that is annually renewable and convertible into a permanent life policy, without providing evidence of insurability.

A young couple typically buys term insurance in their twenties to cover the possibility of loss of income and create funds to pay off a mortgage, or pay for college education. But 30 years later, when that term policy expires, it might be difficult to arrange new insurance to cover estate planning needs. That's why you should always buy term that is convertible into cash value life.

Cash value policies become more complicated. Some policy designs allow you to change the amount of coverage or annual premium, depending on your financial circumstances. Other cash value policies project that by paying larger premiums in the early years, the interest or investment buildup within the policy will cover premiums when you are older. But many of those projections were made when interest rates were at far higher levels. These days, some insurance policy owners are suddenly finding out that, because of years of lower interest rates credited to their policies, they'll owe huge additional annual premiums to keep their insurance in force.

If you have a cash value policy, immediately contact your insurance company for a current projection of cash values, called an *in-force ledger*, to see how long you must keep paying premiums and how large those payments are now projected to be. You don't want to be hit with huge premium increases just when you're planning to retire and might not qualify for a different policy. To get a free life insurance audit of existing policies go to **www.amsterdamfinancial.com**.

Keep Life Insurance Outside Your Estate

In estate planning, the *ownership* of the insurance counts as much as the beneficiary. If you purchased—and own—the life insurance policy, then the proceeds are considered part of your estate even though your named beneficiary receives the payout tax free. That value of your life insurance could increase your estate into the realm of estate taxes.

The answer, in many cases, is to have the insurance policy owned by an *irrevocable life insurance trust*, where it will be considered outside of your estate. Then you can gift money to the trust each year, allowing the independent trustees to use the cash to pay the premiums on the insurance. Remember, you can gift $11,000 a year (and your spouse can gift an additional $11,000) to the trust or to anyone else, outside the combined estate and gift tax calculations. That will allow for the purchase of a sizeable policy, yet keep the ultimate proceeds out of your taxable estate. The one drawback is that you can't personally access any cash that builds inside the policy owned by the trust; so it's important to consult a professional for the appropriate insurance policy design.

If you're not sure who owns your life insurance policy, contact your insurance agent before meeting with your estate planner. You can't just transfer your existing policy into an irrevocable trust. If you die within three years of the transfer, it will be considered part of your estate. But if you don't qualify for a new policy, the transfer might be something you'd rather do now than later. Again, you need professional advice. Just be sure to bring up this topic.

Changing Policies

You may have purchased your life insurance policy years ago. If so, now is the time to check on its current cash value, as well as the ownership and beneficiary. As the owner of the policy, you can change the beneficiary. (That's why I recommend that all divorced spouses who have a court order requiring life insurance to be purchased become the *owner* of the policy on their ex-spouse's life. Then he or she cannot change the beneficiary!) Make sure the beneficiary is appropriately named as part of your new estate plan, and never name a minor child as the beneficiary of a life insurance policy.

It's possible that your existing life insurance policy has not kept pace in design or returns with currently offered policies. But you'll need an independent appraisal to make sure there are better policies available and that you'll qualify for premium rates. If you decide to switch, you can move the cash value from one policy into another by doing a *1035 exchange*—a tax-free transfer of funds between policies. There may be a period of one or two years in which the new policy is contestable by the insurance company should you die suddenly. Never switch from an existing policy to a new one without double-checking prices, terms, and tax consequences.

SPOUSES AND ESTATE PLANNING

My favorite form of estate planning is just to leave everything to your spouse. It's the one simple thing in the very complicated estate tax code: *Assets left to a spouse at death are not subject to estate taxes.* That would be a perfect solution—except that when the surviving spouse dies, the entire remaining estate is subject to taxes. And by that time the estate might be large enough to take a big tax hit.

Estate planners have devised some interesting ways to take advantage of the estate tax exemption listed in Table 18.1 earlier in this chapter. They create two trusts. One, often known as the credit shelter trust, is funded by an amount equal to the estate tax exemption in the year of death. Since that exemption amount will change over time, planners are careful not to list a specific amount, but only "the amount of the exemption."

The surviving spouse cannot be trustee of the credit shelter trust, but he or she can obtain income from it and, if necessary, dig into the principal of the trust. If the surviving spouse doesn't use those assets, at his or her death they will pass directly to the children or other heirs that were specified when the trust was created.

The second trust, set up for the balance of the estate, is typically left to the surviving spouse, who will not be required to pay estate taxes. There is actually no requirement that these assets be placed in trust for the surviving spouse and no tax benefit to doing so. They could easily be given outright. But that would make the assets vulnerable in case a surviving spouse remarries or is a spendthrift.

Spouses should read carefully the restrictions placed on the assets left to them in this second trust, often called the "marital trust." They may be unable to make withdrawals over a certain amount, unable to change investment managers, or unable to change the terms of what happens to the money after the surviving spouse dies. While these provisions may be helpful in second marriages to ensure that children from a first marriage are protected, they can be very limiting. That's why both spouses need to participate in the planning process. Ask a lot of what-if questions along the way, and keep asking until you understand the answers.

CHOOSING AN ESTATE PLANNER

After considering the basic planning issues outlined in this chapter, you are ready to meet with an estate planner. If you've moved to another state since you created your plan, you should have it revised to meet the laws of your new state of residence. You'll need a specialist—an attorney who may be part of a large law firm or a sole practitioner. You can consult your state bar association, but it's usually better to get a personal reference. Sometimes the trust department of a local bank will be willing to give you a list of estate attorneys. Or you can ask business associates or friends. Set up a meeting, and come prepared to ask and to answer questions.

If you don't feel comfortable with a particular attorney, back out and start over with someone else. You're dealing with your most personal issues—not only assets, but also emotional issues that have to do with trusting your spouse, your children, and your attorney—so you want to choose an estate planner whose advice you can trust. Your attorney will help you decide how to carry out your wishes within the law. He or she will have experience with the future impact of decisions rendered today.

Don't let the expense deter you. Depending on where you live, you'll probably get the basic estate planning documents for about $1,500. But if your situation is complicated, with significant assets and complex distribution plans, you might spend several thousand dollars. Whatever the price, it's worth it, not only in the taxes you'll avoid, but also in peace of mind. It's worth it to create a plan that keeps your family intact and well cared for, while avoiding family fights that mar your legacy.

So, no matter what your age or financial situation, I ask you to start considering these issues now. It pays to plan while you can! And once you've made your plan, tell your family members that it exists. That could open the door for a discussion with your parents about their own plans. They may not know how to broach the subject with you—their adult children—so you can take the first step. You also owe it to your children to let them know that your affairs are in order and to tell them where you have left instructions in the event of your death.

ESTATE PLANNING CHECKLIST

- Find a qualified attorney. Ask your bank trust department, wealthy friends, and the state bar association for referrals.
- Decide who will be your co-trustee or successor trustee for your revocable living trust.
- Decide who will act as guardian for your minor children if you and your spouse die together in an accident.

- Decide who will act for you in the health-care power of attorney.
- Decide who will make the decision to enact your living will (pull the plug).
- Contact each IRA, 401(k), or 403(b) plan provider and ask to check the name of the beneficiary you have designated. (*Hint:* Do this *after* your estate planning session, which might lead you to reconsider who gets what.)
- Evaluate the ownership and the beneficiaries of your life insurance policies. If you have minor children, make sure you have established the proper trust relationship if they are life insurance beneficiaries.
- Consider carefully the issue of who gets what. Remember, dividing an estate equally might not be "fair," but dividing an estate unequally is asking for discord.
- Make a list of where all important documents can be found, in case of emergency. List the name and phone number of your professional advisers: attorney, physicians, accountant, insurance agent, and financial planner. Give location of your cemetery deed and funeral instructions. Be sure to include the name and number of the estate planning attorney who has a copy of your Revocable Living Trust. Then leave this basic information—not necessarily the details of your assets or bequests—in a location where your spouse, child, or successor trustee could easily access it if you are incapacitated.

Resources

To understand more about the emotional consequences of your estate plan, as well as the legal implications, I highly recommend:

The Family Fight: Planning to Avoid It, by Les Kotzer and Barry Fish (Continental Atlantic, 2002). **www.family-fight.com**

CONCLUSION

Those are the Savage Numbers. They take you from midlife crisis through the reading of your will. You *can* plan ahead if you refuse to be intimidated by the unknown.

You *can* know with reasonable certainty how much you need to save for the retirement you want and how much you'll need to continue earning in retirement to supplement those savings. You can know with reasonable certainty how to invest your savings—ranging from immediate lifetime annuities to income funds to conservative and aggressive stock funds. And you can know with reasonable certainty how much you can withdraw every year without running out of money in your lifetime.

Notice the words *reasonable certainty*. That's not the kind of absolute certainty you'd need to convict someone of a crime. But it is far better than the guesswork you get from pencil-and-paper calculations or even from the myriad online calculators at financial services web sites. This reasonable certainty derives from projections that are based on historic data, with the same modeling techniques statisticians and scientists use to do everything from sending a spaceship to Mars to decoding the human genome. The calculations are not always perfect, but they're far better than closing your eyes and making a wish.

It's up to us as individuals, and as the baby boomer generation, to face the challenge of planning for our own new world of retirement. We're a generation that has always wanted more of everything. It's something to be proud of because that desire and energy helped move America into the twenty-first century as the strongest country in history.

Don't be afraid. We in the baby boomer generation have always refused to be intimidated, and we have changed the world to acknowledge our massive presence. We've explored space and expanded medicine. We embraced computer technology and physical fitness as symbols of our dominance. And now we will conquer the challenges of living longer and living well.

Instead of worrying about running out of time and money, we need to plan to enhance our financial future. We've never focused on the negatives. We've always focused on the opportunities. Retirement planning is just one more opportunity to leave our mark on history. But we must all take action now. If too many of us fail to plan, our children will carry the tax burden and the social costs of our huge, aging generation.

That's not a legacy I want to leave, and I hope you share my views. It's a personal responsibility to look around the corner and to take advantage of the simple and inexpensive planning techniques that can help us make our money last as long as we do. We can manage the Savage Number. And that's The Savage Truth!

ACKNOWLEDGMENTS

Years of experience have brought me to the point where I could write this book—not only my *own* experiences, but also the generously shared knowledge of true experts in their own fields. In this era of instant access, I urge you to visit their web sites to learn more about their concepts and services.

This book relies heavily on the Monte Carlo analysis tools that Dr. Sam Savage of Stanford University made understandable for me. What a surprise to find we shared not only the same last name but also the same fascination with the possibilities of numbers. I highly recommend his web site (**www.drsamsavage.com**), which will walk you through the concept. And I hereby predict he will follow Dr. William Sharpe in receiving a Nobel Prize one day for his work in this field.

In another realm, I offer a special thank you to Susan McGory, who, in her former role as chief operating officer of CNA Life and Long-Term Care Insurance, first invited me inside the industry and then continued to share her knowledge as I wrote this book. Similarly, Murray and Brian Gordon of Maga Ltd. (**www.magaltc .com**) have been my constant guides through the complexity of policy issues—especially when I purchased my own and my parents' policies. And industry expert Claude Thau (**www.targetins.com**)

was more than generous with his perspective, comments, and contacts. Thanks also to Gail Steingold of Burling Insurance (**www.bigltc.com**).

I am grateful to the major companies in the long term-care insurance industry for offering their research and support in my mission to alert the baby boomer generation to a potential financial crisis. Special thanks go to Christine Bonney and Joyce Ruddock of MetLife, Buck Stinson of Genworth Financial, and Scott Williams of John Hancock.

When it comes to historical information on the stock market, Ibbotson Associates (**www.Ibbotson.com**) is the acknowledged leader, and for years I've called upon Alexa Auerbach there to create (and recreate) graphic market pictures that are worth a thousand words. Grady Durham of Monticello Associates in Denver, Colorado, allowed me to use valuable research he provides primarily to his institutional pension fund clients. Dallas Salisbury of the Employee Benefit Research Institute (**www.EBRI.org**) was a great source for information gleaned from a decade of surveys about retirement confidence. Finance professor Moshe Milevsky of York University in Toronto and Anna Rappaport of Mercer Consulting turned mathematical formulas into English for me.

Over the years, I have continued to rely on advice from experts who always are willing to take my column deadline calls: Jack Fischer (**www.amsterdamfinancial.com**) and Byron Udell (**www.accuquote .com**) for life insurance; Michael Hartz (**www.kmzr.com**) and Janna Dutton (**www.duttonelderlaw.com**) in the field of estate planning; Jeffrey Oster (**Jeffrey.Oster@RaymondJames.com**), a true honest voice in the world of annuities; Hugh McHaffie, annuity expert at MetLife; Peter Bell, president of the National Reverse Mortgage Lenders Association (**www.reversemortgage.org**); and Pat Donohue, jumbo reverse expert, at **pdonohue@rlca.com**. Bill Brodsky, chairman and CEO of the Chicago Board Options Exchange (**www.cboe.com**), and Mark Wolfinger, author of several books on the subject, brought my early experiences as a floor trader on the CBOE into focus for current options opportunities.

The financial services companies mentioned in this book are among the leaders in offering cutting-edge advice and technology to the baby boomer generation. They were not only supportive of my goals, but understanding of my need to remain independent. I particularly must thank Chris Repetto of Intuit, parent company of Quicken, who has been my contact and support there for many years. And it took a double-team at Morningstar.com to keep up with my requests—sincere appreciation to Kathy Panagopoulos and Margaret Kirch Cohen. At **www.FinancialEngines.com**, Asma Emneina grants my requests cheerfully, always, and Dr. William Sharpe is an inspiration.

Judy Wicks at Checkfree became a friend as well as expert adviser on the subject of online bill payments. Peter Gottlieb is always ready with wise stock market investment advice (**PGottlieb @NSIMC.com**). And IRA expert Ed Slott (**www.IRAhelp.com**) has been another generous adviser.

The mutual fund industry is a driving force in investor education, and its aggressive competition in providing the latest in knowledge and tools for the individual is, in my opinion, the most optimistic reason to believe that baby boomers will enjoy a comfortable retirement. Special thanks go to Steve Norwitz of T. Rowe Price, John Woerth of Vanguard, and Cynthia Egan of Fidelity.

I thank the readers of my *Chicago Sun-Times* personal finance column (and Creators Syndicate) for their thought-provoking questions, which have frequently turned into column ideas and fodder for this book. And I thank my *Sun-Times* editor, Dan Miller, for making sure those columns are tightly focused. My colleagues at the Chicago Mercantile Exchange (where I was once a trader and am now a member of the board of directors) have ensured that I am focused on the futures. Special appreciation to Leo Melamed.

My thanks to the editorial staff at Wiley, and especially for the support of Debra Englander, Greg Friedman, and Mary Daniello. Most important, Patricia Stahl has copy-edited each of my four books with incredible patience and understanding. I once thanked her for her "sharp pencil and even sharper mind." To that, I now add thanks for her loyalty and generosity of spirit. Carol Genis is a good friend and great attorney.

I now know why every author thanks family and friends. It's supposed to make up for the time and attention given to the manuscript and research. They accept without question the fact that they'll hear the click of the keyboard while they try to stay in touch by phone! My list of family and friends has grown shorter over the years, but no less dear. I thank them all and point with special pride, once again, to my son, Rex Savage, whose financial expertise is acknowledged by his peers and who is my greatest source of satisfaction.

A final note: Because tax laws and financial products are constantly changing, I invite you to visit my web site, **www.TerrySavage.com**, where you can read my latest columns and where I make every effort to answer e-mails sent to: **terry@terrysavage.com**.

INDEX